Elizabeth Audu

Approved by GOD?

How to serve God and live doing
His will as commanded

Elizabeth Audu

Approved by
GOD?

How to serve God and live doing
His will as commanded

MEREO
Cirencester

Mereo Books

1A The Wool Market Dyer Street Cirencester Gloucestershire GL7 2PR
An imprint of Memoirs Publishing www.mereobooks.com

Approved by God?: 978-1-86151-658-9

First published in Great Britain in 2016
by Mereo Books, an imprint of Memoirs Publishing

The address for Memoirs Publishing Group Limited can be found at
www.memoirspublishing.com

The Memoirs Publishing Group Ltd Reg. No. 7834348

The Memoirs Publishing Group supports both The Forest Stewardship Council®
(FSC®) and the PEFC® leading international forest-certification organisations. Our
books carrying both the FSC label and the PEFC® and are printed on FSC®-certified
paper. FSC® is the only forest-certification scheme supported by the leading
environmental organisations including Greenpeace. Our paper procurement policy
can be found at www.memoirspublishing.com/environment

Typeset in 12/18pt Century Schoolbook
by Wiltshire Associates Publisher Services Ltd. Printed and bound in Great Britain
by Printondemand-Worldwide, Peterborough PE2 6XD

CONTENTS

———◇◇◇———

Dedication

Acknowledgements

About the Author

Introduction

DEDICATION

To give praise, honour,
glory to the Almighty God.
This book is dedicated to
God the Father,
God the Son,
and
God the Holy Spirit.
Without Him, this work would not
have been possible.
Thank you Lord!

ACKNOWLEDGEMENTS

I give all the glory and honour to the Creator of heaven and earth, whose grace and mercy has given me the opportunity and the strength to be a useful vessel and Kingdom builder.

Special thanks to the fearfully and wonderfully covenanted children of the Most High God that the Lord has given unto me. I thank you all, because, without the family support and encouragement, this book would not have been birthed.

I honour our Mother-in-Israel where I gave my life to Christ as a born-again Christian, Bishop

Bolanle Odeleke Founder and General Overseer of (Power Pentecostal Church). The Power of God never fails. Your Ministry has brought about numerous Kingdom generals; you are highly appreciated.

Deepest appreciation to Pastors Gabriel and Mrs Ilori of Christ Gospel Church London, may the Lord strengthen and uphold you till the end. Thanks for your kindness.

My profound gratitude goes to Prophet Johnson and Pastor Mrs Akinfenwa of Voice of Prophecy UK, I say thank you for your support.

My grateful thanks to my Local Assembly before I was called into the Ministry; the RCCG Royal Connections (RC). Appreciation to my Pastors, the Senior Pastors David and Dr Grace Sola-Oludoyi. All the Pastorate and members of R.C., I salute you.

I am very grateful to the leadership of the Redeemed Christian Church of God under the leadership of the General Overseer of the Redeemed Christian Church (RCCG) Pastor Enoch Adeboye. I am indebted to the Principal of Christ The Redeemer College London, Pastor Daniel Akhaemazea, and all the Lecturers at the bible college where I studied. I am forever grateful for the Kingdom values and divine transformation impacted on me.

My sincere appreciation goes to the Senior Pastor Janet Adedipe of RCCG (Redemption Parish), for speaking the Word of Truth while I was serving during my pastoral placement. I say thank you, and to all the ministers, including the children's department.

I am thankful to Bishop David Oyedepo for undiluted teaching like the wisdom principles, living by faith etc. These have contributed immensely to my spirituality. I am also grateful to the Winner families, both home and abroad.

I am deeply grateful to Prophet Lanre and Lady Evangelist Mrs Olotu of International Christian Association you are very much appreciated for your support, including the entire ICA members.

I acknowledge the Ministers of Night Vigil Forum in London, all my friends, families, helpers of destinies in one capacity or the other.

I would like to acknowledge the many authors whose books have over the years been invaluable sources of knowledge and inspiration to me.

To my biological parents, Pa Joseph (RIP) and Mrs Okononfua, who nurtured me and my siblings in the way of the Lord, able to give us a comprehensive education, especially with my being a woman, which was not the norm as of that era. I say thank you Sir and Ma. I also acknowledge your invaluable contributions to my life and children when faced with the unexpected events of life. Thank you for being there.

My beloved spouse, honest and caring helper of destiny, Sir Samuel O. Audu (RIP): there is nothing that can replace your absence. My most reliable and loving immediate junior brother who pushed me to excellence by his inspiration and his modelling, Dr Willy Emmanuel Okononfua (RIP).

I thank God for the spiritual children the Lord has brought on my journey and the entire member of the Compassionate Act International Outreach in the UK, Africa, and all over the world. May the power in the blood of Jesus Christ always be a shield, providing peace, prosperity, and a refuge, both in the physical and spiritual dimensions, in the Name of Jesus Christ of Nazareth Amen.

My gratitude towards everyone who will be affected by this book. May God bless you all in the Mighty Name of Jesus Christ Amen.

ABOUT THE AUTHOR

—━◁◇▷━—

Elizabeth L. Audu was born in Lagos, Nigeria, originated from Edo State (Ishan) Irua/Uromi, and is a former staff member of the Nigerian Television Authority (NTA), Victoria Island, Lagos. She has since lived in the United Kingdom for many years, as a Registered Nurse and Community Practitioner. Elizabeth holds a Diploma of Higher Education in Adult Nursing and degree in Bachelor of Science (Hons) in Health Promotion and Public Health. She is able to impact the community in promoting health and well-being of the family. She attained a Diploma in Christian Ministries at the National Open College Network and a degree in Bachelor of Arts in Pastoral Theology from Trinity College, at Newburgh in the State of Indiana, U.S.A. She is a Pastor, a motivational speaker, and a counsellor in the areas of prayers.

To purchase this book
Please contact:
07525852175
07534794826
07417577864
Email: Pstmrselizabethaudu@mail.com

INTRODUCTION

———⟨⟨⟨⟩⟩⟩———

What is approval?

Approval is the action of approving of something, giving a favourable opinion. For example, a seal of approval is an indication that something is officially accepted or given a satisfactory of authorization (Concordance Dictionary). However, the Spiritual perspectives of an Approval are metaphorically used as the testing of the Christian's faith. According to 1st Peter 1:7:

That the trial of your faith, being much more precious than of gold that perisheth, though it be tried with fire, might be found unto praise and honour and glory at the appearing of Jesus Christ.

Hence (2nd Corinthians 5:9): **Wherefore we labour, that, whether present or absent, we may be accepted of him.**

In other to please Him, saints ought to be doing things that makes God happy. He takes pleasure in His people. The Scripture declared that humanity was created in the image and likeness of God (Genesis 1:26):

And God said, "let us make man in our image, after our likeness and let them have dominion over the fish of the sea, and over the fowl of the air, and over the cattle, and over all the earth, and over every creeping thing that creepeth upon the earth".

All others reproduce after their kind. Man was the only one made in the image of God, but the Creator of mankind was unhappy with His creation as pre-planned, doing things in their own ways as (2nd Corinthians 5:10) affirmed: **For we must all appear before the judgment seat of Christ; that every one may receive the things done in his body, according to that he hath done, whether it be good or bad.**

There is a book of reckoning because everyone shall stand in God's presence to give account. Except we strive hard to do His will in order to please Him before an approval is obtained. Christianity is of the Jews, but The Saviour paid a sacrificial offering for humanity to both the Jews and the Gentiles. He is a universal God.

Jesus Christ is the only judge (Roman 14:12): **So then every one of us shall give account of himself to God**. Therefore, specified in 1st Peter 4:5: **Who shall give account to him that is ready to judge the quick and the dead.**

For that reason, pleasing God relocates you from the realm of carnality to spirituality of God. To obtain God's approval is to live a well- pleasing lifestyle, because a man in the flesh cannot please God and the wages of sin is death. God was able to declare to His only begotten Son as stated in Mark 1:11: **And there came a voice from heaven, saying, Thou art my beloved Son, in whom I am well pleased.**

One testimony you must have is that you pleased God because there is a heavenly certificate of approval attached for doing His will. Everyone who pleases God gets a divine promotion. Some of our patriarchs like Enoch, Abraham etc. and Jesus were accepted. You can be too. To what extent have you pleased God? If we do, you and I will care about everything God cares about. You will obey Him totally, because partial obedience is disobedience.

Colossians 1:27 stated: **To whom God would make known what is the riches of the glory of this mystery among the Gentiles; which is Christ in you, the hope of glory.**

Thus there is no reason why believers cannot please God as much as Jesus did. We have been born again spiritually, made in His image, He lives in us. We have been given His righteousness, filled with the power of the Holy Spirit, possessed of all the capacity that Jesus Christ had during His earthly ministry. He was fully dedicated to God's will, a sinless Christ. He prayed many times, He ministered all day and prayed all night, yet He had flesh and blood like you. So there was an element of crucifying the flesh involved, He (die-to-self) and yes to His Father. Saints, we need to live a righteous living, dared to be different positively, and choose the heavenly pathway.

How can approval be obtained?

To obtain God's approval you must go through tests and trials in total obedience to His word, keeping the commandments and fellowshipping with Him in love. According to 1st John 2:3-6:

3 And hereby we do know that we know him, if we keep his commandments.

4 He that saith, I know him, and keepeth not his commandments, is a liar, and the truth is not in him.

5 But whoso keepeth his word, in him verily is the love of God perfected: hereby know we that we are in him.

6 He that saith he abideth in him ought himself also so to walk, even as he walked.

Disobedience always ends in tragedy or pain. Hence, involvement in obedience to God's commandment provides increasingly clear evidence of a true believer. The love for God is not something mystical, but practical, that finds expression in approachable to God's commandment. As an individual claiming to know God in the reality, and having a fellowshipping with Him without obedient, is not a true believer. Most significantly, the promise of forgiveness is the truth and Jesus Christ is the atoning sacrifice for the sin of humanity.

If a man say, I love God, and hateth his brother, he is a liar; for he that loveth not his

brother whom he hath seen, how can he love God whom he hath not seen?

You can obtain approval from God by abiding to Kingdom Principles in order to please Him, must be ready for tests/trials. Although, you can be classified as an enemy by close friends and families, just because you stepped out to please your maker. Normally, pleasing Him can make you displeased yourself. Even people that surround you might be thinking you are losing your mind, but have no idea you are obeying the voice of God. The question is, are you prepared to pay the price? Saints, you need to be disciplined doing the will of God that will enable His approval.

Jesus paid that price. He dumped His personal aspiration for that of His Father's will.

This was the birth of faith, in the account of Matthew 3:16-17:

16 **And Jesus when he was baptized, went up straightway out of the water, and, lo, the heavens were opened unto him, and he saw the Spirit of God descending like a dove, and lighting upon him.**

17 **And lo a voice from heaven, saying, "This is my beloved Son, in whom I am well pleased."**

As Jesus Christ was being baptized, immediately He came out of the river waters, the Spirit of God descended on Him, then the above voice came from God's Kingdom to His beloved Son. Saints, whatever we can do so that God can be happy with us as an individual. In our routine lifestyles, His requirement is for us to live a holy and righteous life for us to obtain His approval. Consequently, as soon as you become a born-again Christian spontaneously you bear the genetics of Jesus Christ, and without the baptism of water and of the Holy Spirit you cannot hear His voice, nor yield to His commandments, nor attain his acceptance of approval for His kingdom. If God could not spare His only begotten son who was (sinless Christ) and was released as a sacrificial offering to humanity, saints have no option than to abide in doing His will and living a life pleasing unto God.

His food is what He enjoyed doing the most for making God happy. Even when the task at hand involved giving His life, He indebted as specified - Isaiah 53:3-5:

3   He is despised and rejected of men; a man of sorrows, and acquainted with grief: and we hid as it were our faces from him; he was despised; and we esteemed him not.

4   Surely he hath borne our griefs, and carried our sorrows: yet we did esteem him stricken, smitten of God, and afflicted.

5   But he was wounded for our transgressions, he was bruised for our iniquities: the chastisement of our peace was upon him; and with his stripes we are healed.

The severity of the description of Jesus Christ suffering from the New Testament account at the Garden of Gethsemane, when His will crossed God's heart. Nevertheless He gave all (surrendered His life) as He professed:

"Jesus said unto them, My meat is to do the will of him that sent me, and to finish his work" (John 4:34).

Jesus demonstrated love without prejudice by breaking the barrier. His assignment was to execute what His Father commanded Him to do.

He need to work closer among the Samaritans, the lost souls, unbeliever for fruitful results that was His meat.

The salvation of sinners is the will of God, and abide to the instruction given to Him. Jesus was sent into the world for this purpose, to bring people to God, to know Him and for God to be happy with Him. So, He made this work His business and delight. As nothing could be more grateful to Him than moral deeds to people whenever and wherever invited where He is opportune to manifest His sovereignty was his meat always. The work is to preach the gospel (soul winning) for His kingdom that was His Fathers work, and His will.

This is applicable to the saint who lives by faith, that they have meat to eat which others knew not of, or joy which a stranger does not know about. Our Lord Jesus is our role model. It is for us to emulate Him such as being diligence, delight and pleasure in what you are called to do; also to be faithful and perseverance not only minding to do for effectiveness, but aiming to finish well.

The question for us is: are you operating under God's agenda?

The conversation between Jesus and the

Samaritan Woman from the previous (John 4:1-26; & 34-37). The disciples wondered how their master could have descended so low to communicate with such a poor contemptible woman, forgetting how dreadful they themselves were before they came in contact with Christ Himself. Noticeably, this woman forgot her errand to the well, why she went to fetch water: she left her water-pot and called her friends and neighbours thus, propagating the gospel of Christ to her people. Do you realize that no matter who you are, you and I have got an assignment to accomplish for kingdom of Heavenly business. Your world is awaiting you, and you got no excuse. That woman was nobody within the community, but when she advertised Christ people listened to her because she dared not fabricate any false information because her life would be at risk. She was accepted by Christ, turned her mess into message as she forged ahead and proclaimed Christ, while she became the first Lady Evangelist in the Bible.

Although Jesus Christ is the only Begotten of the Father, while believers fall under the adoptive sons. In that circumstance, Jesus does watch how faithful you were to Him, and if you really believed that He is your Lord and Saviour. Therefore, believers like you and me have been tested in one capacity or the other, so it is basic that obedience in doing His will is the reality that helps us in diverse ways as it provides proof that we know God, abide to His commandment, then grow deeper in Him (John 14: 15-24). Hence, whosoever lives to have an intimacy in fellowshipping with God definitely will live as Jesus lived to please His Father.

Obedience is better than sacrifice (1st Samuel 13:12-14).

When you obey, you thus adhered to His commandment for Him to be pleased with you. From the Old Testament perspectives, the Lord gave the Ten Commandments through His servant Moses (Exodus 20: 1-17), while from the New Testament views it was embedded in love, which was the greatest commandment (John 3:16) "Jesus is Love".

For God so loved the world that he gave his only begotten Son, that whosoever believeth in him should not perish, but have everlasting life.

If you love, you will not go against the will of God.

Nevertheless, there are examples like Enoch, who did not see death but was translated because he pleased God (Hebrew 11:5). Abraham the father of faith, even Noah, found favour during the time of atrocities as it were in this era (Genesis 6:8; Hebrew 11:7). The same is applicable to Jesus Christ, who is our role model.

This book came into existence by the power of the Holy Spirit, which inspired me to put it in writing as instructed as a "Wake-Up" word of knowledge some years back. Due to one thing or the other it could not be written but a few weeks ago suddenly the Lord ignited my spirit. Within that week, I received messages directly from different individual personalities to proceed to do what God had instructed, although I was disturbed I just got a very lucrative contract, but I had to make a quick decision and abandon other things to obey this mandate. Saints, I implored you to harken to the voice of the Lord as He commanded you towards any steps concerning this great commission.

As you read through this book, may the power of the Holy Spirit incubate your life, be transformed, and in obedience to His commandment, doing His will, may you be accepted for His approval in Jesus Name Amen. Be blessed!

This book will be demonstrating some principles for obtaining approval in the following chapters such as: How we can honour God in Worship, Living by faith, obedience to God commandment and giving/offering which are all mandatory for His commendation.

Chapter One

WORSHIPPING GOD

—◦◦◦—

To worship is to bow down in reverence, the totality in the act of honouring God. King David the Psalmist wrote most of the Book of Psalms for worshipping, praising, giving thanks and appreciating God. He was a man full of praising God all the time, the secret behind his success, as praise is another avenue into worship. Hence, the psalms are the literature of worship and the most noticeable feature is praise. Singing is meant to move us into praise. It provides a medium for the expression of emotions by means of music

1

whereby we express joy in our thanksgiving. The greatest blessing that a man can offer God is to be thankful to Him and praise Him routinely.

Demonstration of worship, according to the Scripture, is through physical expressions. We find a series of physical postures in relation to worship: lying, prostrate, standing, kneeling, lifting of hands, clapping hands, bowing the head, dancing and wearing sackcloth and ashes. Thus we are to surrender unto God all our bodies as well as all the rest of our being in obeisance as an act of honour and worship towards God.

There is a difference between thanksgiving and praising God. Under normal circumstances, you can thank people when they have showed kindness to you and thanked them for what they have done. Hence, we praise people not necessarily for what they did but because of who they are, their achievements and what they can do. Thus the recognition of their talent or capabilities in their endeavours.

According to the Scripture declared by Jesus Christ (Matthew 21:16b): *Yea; have ye never read, OUT OF THE MOUTH OF BABES AND SUCKLINGS THOU HAST PERFECTED PRAISE?*

Jesus quoted the scripture from Psalms 8:2. As newborn children of the eternal kingdom, He revealed to us one of our roles on earth, building the throne of the King through praise. The praise of God is in your lips; your mouth carries the throne of the King of the earth. And you can crown Him anywhere, any time by lifting your voice in praise consistently (Psalms 95:6): *O come, let us worship and bow down; let us kneel before the LORD our maker.*

Saints, we can worship God in diverse ways, for example in praising and thanksgiving, thus activating His sovereign power. For example in some cultures, during important events such as weddings, naming ceremonies, burial, etc. they entertained guests with an artist accompanied by musical instruments like talking drums. While the host is dancing and rejoicing, there are some commentary and praises that goes with the orchestra while he or she is happy with those accolades. Could you imagine if people know how to engage their guests with entertainments in conjunction with appreciation; why not much more for our Heavenly Father that deserves all the glory, honour, takes pleasure in worshiping God.

This was confirmed by Revelation 4:10-11:

10 *The four and twenty elders fall down before him that sat on the throne, and worship him that liveth for ever and ever, and cast their crowns before the throne, saying,*

11 *Thou are worthy, O Lord, to receive glory and honour and power: for thou hast created all things, and for thy pleasure they are and were created.*

We can ponder on the above scripture. All heaven worships the Father, while the angels extol His character, and the elders within the congregation praise His creative power. Hence He is routinely worthy of our praise. We thank Him for what He has done, doing, even about to do. It gives Him splendour and acknowledged that He is a holy God, the Creator of all being, and He is sovereign.

The power of praise can never be underestimated. It brings deliverance and healing and also refreshes the body and mind. Wherever praise is God's presence is awesome; there and wherever the spirit of the Lord is, definitely there is liberty (1st Samuel 16:14-23):

14 But the Spirit of the LORD departed from Saul, and an evil spirit from the LORD troubled him.

15 And Saul's servants said unto him, Behold now, an evil spirit from God troubleth thee.

16 Let our Lord now command thy servants, which are before thee, to seek out a man, who is a cunning player on a harp: and it shall come to pass, when the evil spirit from God is upon thee, that he shall play with his hand, and thou shalt be well.

17 And Saul said unto his servants, Provides me now a man that can play well, and bring him to me.

18 Then answered one of the servants, and said, Behold, I have seen a son of Jesse the Bethlehemite, that is cunning in playing, and a mighty valiant man, and a man of war, and prudent in matters, and a comely person, and the LORD is with him.

19 Wherefore, Saul sent messengers unto Jesse, and said, Send me David thy son, which is with the sheep.

20 And Jesse look an ass laden with bread, and a bottle of wine, and a kid, and sent them by David his son unto Saul.

21 And David came to Saul, and stood before him; and he loved him greatly; and he became his armour-bearer.

22 And Saul sent to Jesse, saying, Let David, I pray thee, stand before me; for he hath found favour in my sight.

23 And it came to pass, when the evil spirit from God was upon Saul, that David took a harp, and played with is hand: so Saul was refreshed, and was well, and the evil spirit departed from him.

The incident was when King Saul was suffering depression, and then David was invited as a Praise Worshipper of God to the palace. After the musical exercises, he was soothed, and the evil spirit departed from Saul. That is the sole rationale behind praising and worshipping God, and the result is authentic and serves as a deliverance device.

Furthermore, there was an event that took place when the Lord commanded Joshua when they were faced with challenges (Joshua 6:13-15):

13 And seven priests bearing seven trumpets of rams horns before the ark of the Lord went on continually, and blew with the trumpets: and the armed men went before them; but the rearward came after the ark of the LORD, the priests going on, and blowing with the trumpets.

14 And the second day they compassed the city once, and returned into the camp: so they did six days.

15 And it came to pass on the seventh day, that they rose early about the dawning of the day, and compassed the city after the same manner seven times: only on that day they compassed the city seven times.

God instructed Joshua to tell them to walk round the city of Jericho and on the seventh day with a shout of Thunderous Hallelujah, the Wall of Jericho fell down with the commandment of God

(Joshua 6:2-20). Issues dealt with in prolonged prayers without immediate results can automatically have divine intervention in praising God with quality of praise. You then experience manifestations of His powers with positive results. Thus you took a further bold step of action, which is to give God audacious praise, thanking Him for who He is, because He is able.

Furthermore, heaven and earth declared the glory of the Lord (Isaiah 55:12):

For ye shall go out with joy, and be led forth with peace: the mountains and the hills shall break forth before you into singing, and all the trees of the filed shall clap their hands.

As men acknowledge the sovereignty of God, all creatures extol His power; even the stones and trees do praise and worship Him. Saints, you have no reason not to appreciate Him.

Below is one of the psalm of praise towards God declaring His Salvation (Psalm 98:1-9).

God is still incomprehensible in the totality of His person and purpose, as the psalm declared: the coming of the Lord on earth is celebrated as an event of great joy. Hence, it was categorised into three dimensions which are called upon to rejoice (verses 1-3):

1   *O sing unto the Lord a new song; for he hath done marvellous things: his right hand, and his holy arm, hath gotten him the victory.*

2   *The LORD hath made known his salvation: his righteousness hath he openly showed in the sight of the heathen.*

3   *He hath remembered his mercy and his truth toward the house of Israel: all the ends of the earth have seen the salvation of our God.*

While the whole earth proclaimed his sovereignty (verses 4-6):

4   *Make a joyful noise unto the LORD, all the earth: make a loud noise, and rejoice, and sing praise.*

5   *Sing unto the LORD with the harp; with the harp, and the voice of a psalm.*

6   *With trumpets and sound of cornet make a joyful noise before the LORD, the King.*

So also, all nature declared His glory (verses 7-9).

7   *Let the sea roar, and the fullness therefore, the world, and they that dwell therein.*

8   *Let the floods clap their hands: let the hills be joyful together.*

9   *Before the LORD; for he cometh to judge the earth: with righteousness shall he judge the world, and the people with equity.*

Therefore, God is calling all his creatures to worship. It brings God grandeur, and this is what He expected from His creation, the handiwork of the Creator, and we are called to emulate Christ. It is for believers to live holy lifestyles and acknowledge that He is sovereign in every state of affairs. This is clearly stated in the book of 1st Thessalonica 5:18:

In everything give thanks: for this is the will of God in Christ Jesus concerning you.

All disciplined people in the Bible were able to obtained approval in doing His will and live a life pleasing unto God. That is what is expected of believers too. Therefore, praise will keep you in harmony with God. As a king is always loyal to his throne, so believers in close relationships will always be refreshed in the presence of God.

Saints, I will suggest as we enter into God's presence, the first thing is to give Him due thanks and when we depart, to do likewise, as a lifestyle choice. This is because travelling from your home to your destination is worthy of praise for mercy on the journey. Thanksgiving is Heaven's certified material for packaging and presenting requests, as God dwell in praising, He has no choice than to grant the petition (Psalms 100:4)

Enter into his gates with thanksgiving, and into his courts with praise: be thankful unto him, and bless his name.

On a continual basis give Him sacrifice of thanksgiving, He loved to be celebrated (Psalm 145:1-3):

1   *I will extol thee, my God, O king; and
    I will bless thy name for ever and ever.*

2   *Every day will I bless thee; and I will
    praise thy name for ever and ever.*

3   *Great is the LORD, and greatly to be
    praised; and his greatness is
    unsearchable.*

This psalm is recognised for several unique features, including the last Davidic psalm to be called a praise psalm, and the first of the six great praising psalms. He appreciates whom God is in his life; the call to praise and being called to appreciate God on continual basis. He as the King offers four key reasons to praise the Almighty God in the section called 'the reason for praise' (verses 3-20). Saints, we all have reasons to praise Him. The question is, haven't you got reason to praise and thank Him? You might think you have made a demand in prayers of various requests and not being answered. Saints, an example is to enable you to see the breaking of another day, we have to give Him thanks.

Kind David on a continual basis demonstrated how great is God (verse 3); He is gracious and merciful (verses 8-9), and that the Almighty God sustains all who fall (verse 14). May you receive divine grace for sustainment whenever and wherever it is needed. Nevertheless, God is righteous in His ways (verse 17). We should remember that He is a just God.

For example, in the Parable of the Talents, the one with only one talent who was ungrateful without appreciation, he buried the little token that he was giving (Matthew 25:14-30). Jesus was demonstrating to believers the importance of faithful service in doing His will. Also, not to be a slothful and unprofitable servant who never emulates Christ Jesus. Hence he was not portraying a true disciple. Nevertheless, this incident is a warning to learn from previous mistakes that grieved God. He has seen your capability before distribution of your job description. You could have perceived that that little gift of God in you is tiny while you started comparing yourself with another fellow. You are His creation; He knows what you can cope with. That little gift you have been ordained from Heaven for your fulfilment is for you to work on, rather than being discontented and complaining that it is not big enough.

Saints, do you realised that a little smile goes a long way? It is therapeutic and it makes an impact in someone's life. That two-minute phone call to say hello and ask about someone's wellbeing goes a long way in someone's life, but not to gossip. You make the other person smile, then God will put a smile on your own face, that is how it works. No matter how huge or little a gift is, thankfulness and showing appreciation are vital. That ungrateful servant that hid his talent was judged and condemned; we shall not be condemned in Jesus' name.

Furthermore, the Bible recorded the story of Esau, who lost his birthright. He never valued his position as the firstborn. Appreciation means a lot thus: you valued what was given to you by God, no matter how big or small from someone to you, need to be grateful. Esau lost his divine position just for a piece of meal (Genesis 25:29-34):

29   *And Jacob sod pottage: and Esau came from the field, and he was faint:*

30   *And Esau said to Jacob, Feed me, I pray thee, with that same red pottage; for I am faint: therefore was his name called Edom.*

31   *And Jacob said, Sell me this day thy birthright.*

32   *And Esau said, Behold, I am at the point to die: and what profit shall this birthright do to me?*

33   *And Jacob said, Swear to me this day; and he sware unto him: and he sold his birthright unto Jacob.*

*34 Then Jacob gave Esau bread and
pottage of lentils; and he did eat and
drink, and rose up, and went his way:
thus Esau despised his birthright.*

Our destiny shall not be aborted nor destroyed
due to careless or materialist pressures that are
temporary. Although Esau was the first born and
their father's favourite, he lost his birthright and
blessing to his twin brother. Hence there are
temporary phases in life when you experience
challenges, but not for long. It might just be testing
your standing with God. Many believers are into
all sorts of atrocities, for one reason or the other.
Nonetheless, Esau signifies the profane creature
and the non-elected of God according to the
Scripture, for he sold his birthright that shall not
be our lot. May our destiny never be substituted
due to any pressing issues nor when faced with
challenges of life. May God grant us the grace to
stand in faith, persevered and put everything in
prayer to win battles in Jesus name Amen.

The psalm 145 is applicable to believers. It is
for us to emulate Jesus Christ as our role model;
we utilized it as a routine practice of a lifestyle
that can give God splendour that enabled Him

have pleasure with us. It pleases God when we celebrate and acknowledge him, as He loved to be appreciated. Saints, as a parent who expected to be honoured by your own children or your subordinates, we love compliments, and so does God. He is pleased when we are grateful, but grieved if we give no signal of appreciation.

Jesus is the example of whom we need to emulate, He is addicted to appreciating His Father. The Bible states this in various instances, such as the story of the five barley loaves and two small fishes (John 6:11):

And Jesus took the loaves; and when he had given thanks, he distributed to the disciples, and the disciples to them that were set down; and likewise of the fishes as much as they would.

He gave His Father thanks before He made any demand. Another account demonstrates how grateful Jesus is to His Father (John 11:41-42):

41 Then they took away the stone from the place where the dead was laid. And Jesus lifted up his eyes, and said, Father, I thank thee that thou hast heard me.

42 And I knew that thou hearest me always: but because of the people which stand by I said it, that they may believe that thou hast sent me.

During the episode of Lazarus at his Tomb, Jesus gave thanks and watched God for divine intervention. *Father I thank thee that thou hast heard me* (John 11:41b). His father heard him because He made Him happy and proud that with Him all things are possible. Thanksgiving is a tool or weapon of restoration.

As God manifested Himself, many gave their lives to Christ from that hopeless situation while it added value to His kingdom and more souls were saved. Hence, the ability to thank Him in everything, as He gave you the grace. Then your duty is to give Him thanks, either in little or big achievement God has manifested Himself. Let's ponder on the fact that some people have food but cannot eat, while some can eat but have no food. God is not the author of confusion but a solver of problems. He needs to be appreciated, worshipped and adored. We have examples of people who did His will, leaving a life that delighted God before they were accepted.

To obtain approval is for you to do what pleases Him, give God the splendour that you are a son /daughter of His Kingdom. However, if an earthly parent can give children a gift that is not yet purchased because of the child's attitude towards appreciating things in thanking his/her parent ahead, a good parent would go the extra mile to give a quality gift. How much more our Father the Creator of heaven and earth. Hence, we endeavour to live a life pleasing unto God, in doing His will, honouring, praising and thankful to Him; all this makes God happy, that you trust in Him, thereby obtaining his certificate of approval.

The episode that took place at the prison during the earthquake was not intended to deliver Paul but to convert the jailer and his household for them to know that there is God in heaven. God knew that Paul would be released the next day; therefore the earthquake was not merely for Paul and Silas's benefit, but to save souls to His kingdom. The earthquake would have been meaningless had not the jailer heard Paul's testimony in prayer and songs.

Act 16: 25-40 but need to dwell on (verses 25-31)

And at midnight, Paul and Silas prayed and sang praises unto God: and the prisoners heard them.

*26 And suddenly there was a great
     earthquake, so that the foundations of
     the prison were shaken: and
     immediately all the doors were opened,
     and every one's bands were loosed.*

*27 And the keeper of the prison awaking
     out of his sleep, and seeing the prison
     doors open, he drew out his sword, and
     would have killed himself, supposing
     that the prisoners had been fled.*

*28 But Paul cried with a loud voice, saying,
     Do thyself no harm: for we are all here.*

*29 Then he called for a light, and sprang
     in, and came trembling, and fell down
     before Paul and Silas,*

*30 And brought them out, and said, Sirs,
     what must I do to be saved?*

*31 And they said, Believe on the Lord Jesus
     Christ, and thou shalt be saved, and thy
     house.*

Their singing brought about divine intervention
via the earthquake. The significance aspect was
soul-winning. The benefit of singing praises,
worshipping, thankfulness, meant Paul and Silas

were able to use that medium to convert the jailer with his household while they all gave their lives to Christ. There are circumstances that occurred for the manifestation of God's sovereignty. Apostle Paul passionately forged ahead despite persecution and attained his goal in doing the will of God, with a pleasing lifestyle that rewarded him with approval.

God is grateful when we praise and worship him, but grieved when we grumble or complain with an expression of ingratitude. Jesus Christ lived a life pleasing unto God as He declared.

The Father made a declaration:

And lo a voice from heaven, saying, This is my beloved Son, in whom I am well pleased (Matthew 3:17).

This was verbal approval of the ministry of His beloved Son. There can be no doubt that all three persons of the Trinity are actively involved here as distinct persons of the Godhead. He lived in obedience and appreciated His Father; as the Father made the declaration, the Holy Spirit descended, and God the Son was baptised. It was Jesus Christ's lifestyle in doing God's will to live to please Him to gain approval.

Similarly the account of the woman with the alabaster oil (Matthew: 26:6-13):

6   *Now when Jesus was in Bethany, in the house of Simon the leper,*

7   *There came unto him a woman having an alabaster box of very precious ointment, and poured it on his head, as he sat of meat.*

8   *But when his disciples saw it, they hag indignation, saying, To what purpose is this waste?*

9   *For this ointment might have been sold for much, and given to the poor.*

10   *When Jesus understood if, he said unto them, Why trouble ye the woman? For she hath wrought a good work upon me.*

11   *For ye have the poor always with you; but me ye have not always.*

12   *For in that she hath poured this ointment on my body, she did it for my burial.*

13   *Verily I say unto you, Wheresoever this gospel shall be preached in the whole*

world, there shall also this, that this woman hath done, be told for a memorial of her.

This woman honoured and worshipped Christ with her substance, hence according to the scripture her name should be inscribed in the book of remembrance. This was an expensive and precious ointment. This woman spent her money as a sacrificial offering and was recorded for her good work. She poured the ointment on the body of Christ which was symbolic towards Christ's burial; that led towards the gospel of Good News of the Lord's death and resurrection. Jesus foretold a criminal's death, and with that signal under normal circumstances a criminal's burial would mean never having the opportunity of being anointed, but this woman (Mary, sister to Martha and Lazarus) worshipped and adored Christ. She lavishly dignified His body with expensive oil that cost the equivalent of one year's salary for a rural worker.

The question is, what legacy are you leaving behind, or what good deed can you be remembered for? Also, how can you make God happy and be approved of Him? In any thing you do saints, either in singing praises, thanksgiving, bowing down, clapping hands, honouring, reverencing in appreciation, all are ways of worshipping God. God deserved it.

Chapter Two

FAITH

———◦⋈◦———

According to the Scripture (Hebrew 11: 1): ***Now faith is the substance of things hoped for, the evidence of things not seen.***

The book of Hebrew laid emphasises on Faith. Christianity is absolutely worthless without faith, as it is the principal tool for doing exploits in the kingdom, Heb. 11:32-34:

32 ***And what shall I more say? For the time would fail me to tell of Gideon, and of Barak, and of Samson, and of Jephthah; of David also, and Samuel, and of the prophets:***

33 Who through faith subdued kingdoms, wrought righteousness, obtained promises, stopped the mouth of lions.

34 Quenched the violence of fire, escaped the edge of the sword, out of weakness were made strong, waxed valiant in fight, turned to flight the armies of the aliens.

Faith is what enhances believers and allows you to stand in the midst of afflictions, as God is always in control. It is also the splendour of Christianity that always triumphantly generates noble accounts and never dwindling power.

Faith is the master key to a triumphant life with evident. Hence, (Mark 11:22): *And Jesus answering saith unto them, Have faith in God.*

As stated by Jesus, if you have faith as little as the grain of a mustard seed, you can move mountains, and nothing shall be impossible unto you.

Matthew 17:20: *And Jesus said unto them, Because of your unbelief: for verily I say unto you, if ye have faith as a grain of mustard seed, ye shall say unto this mountain, Remove hence to yonder place; and it shall remove; and nothing shall be impossible unto you.*

Faith enables us to function in the realm of God, where nothing shall be impossible. Nevertheless, the validity of faith does not rest on the sincerity of the believer, but on the efficacy of what is believed.

Additionally, the evidence of Faith in which we may not see the object, but do have the evidence, has a visible impact on human technical knowhow. From times past, those who have trusted God have demonstrated the validity of their faith thus: those who followed Jesus all through while they placed their feet on a pathway with no doubt, such as Abraham, Enoch, Noah, Job, Apostle Paul, Queen Esther, Mary Magdalene etc never turned back. Saints, you can do likewise.

Let's look at the book of Hebrew 11 (verses 2-11):

2 *For by it the elders obtained a good report.*

3 *Through faith we understand that the worlds were framed by the word of God, so that things which are seen were not made of things which do appear.*

4   *By faith Abel offered unto God a more excellent sacrifice than Cain, by which he obtained witness that he was righteous, God testifying of his gifts and by it he being dead yet speaketh.*

5   *By faith Enoch was translated that he should not see death; AND WAS NOT FOUND, BECAUSE GOD HAD TRANSLATED HIM; for before his translation he had this testimony, that he pleased God.*

6   *But without faith it is impossible to please him: for he that cometh to God must believe that he is, and that he is a rewarder of them that diligently seek him.*

7   *By faith, Noah, being warned of God of things not seen as yet moved with fear, prepared an ark to the saving of his house; by the which he condemned the world, and because heir of the righteousness which is by faith.*

8   *By faith Abraham, when he was called to go out into a place which he should*

after receive for an inheritance, obeyed; and he went out, not knowing whither he went.

9   *By faith he sojourned in the land of promise, as in a strange country, dwelling in tabernacles with Isaac and Jacob, the heirs with him of the same promise:*

10 *For he looked for a city which hath foundations, whose builder and maker is God.*

11 *Through faith also Sarah herself received strength to conceive seed, and was delivered of a child when she was past age, because she judged him faithful who had promised.*

Abel offered unto God a more excellent sacrifice than Cain. In what way was his sacrifice better? Was is it because his was animal and Cain's vegetable? Or his a first fruit and not Cain's? Or was his with blood and Cain's without? The book of Hebrews and Genesis (4:1-15) demonstrated that it was not the offering that made one acceptable and the other unacceptable. God accepted both grain and animal offerings according to their purposes, but the character of the worshipper made one offering more acceptable than the other, Abel offered his by faith, while Cain was not. Genesis records that even before the rejection of Cain's offering his heart was not right with God (Genesis: 4:7):

If thou doest well, shalt thou not be accepted? And if thou doest not well, sin lieth at the door. And unto thee shall be his desire, and thou shalt rule over him.

The question is, how is your heart and mind with God? It is time to wake up and examine your character and attitude towards one another. Let us arise and do the will of God as commanded and live a life that is pleasing unto God for us to be approved of Him.

Abel, the succeeding child of the human race, had God's witness that he was righteous (Hebrew 11:4):

By faith Abel offered unto God a more excellent sacrifice than Cain, by which he obtained witness that he was righteous, God testifying of his gifts: and by it he being dead yet speaketh.

Abel offered unto God a more excellent sacrifice than Cain. How is Abel's better than Cain's? It was just because Abel offered his by faith, while Cain's heart was not right with God. Abel and his offering were accepted, because his works were righteous.

Leviticus 1:4: ***And he shall put his hand upon the head of the burnt offering; and it shall be accepted for him to make atonement for him.***

There is indication of a man of faith in Abel, while we perceive the carnality of man in Cain (materialism):

1st John 3 12: ***Not as Cain, who was of the wicked one, and slew his brother. And wherefore slew he him? Because his own works were evil, and his brother's righteous.***

Abel offered by faith, Cain did not. Abel had a conscience of sin and acknowledged the effects and Cain did not. How is your mind set towards your neighbour or your brother? This is food for thought.

Hence, according to Ephesians 2:13:

But now in Christ Jesus ye who sometimes were far off are made nigh to God by the blood of Christ

We have boldness to enter the holiest by the blood of Jesus, by a new covenant, which He has consecrated for us and spoken of the blood of righteousness (Hebrew 10:18-22):

18 Now where remission of these is, there is no more offering for sin.

19 Having therefore, brethren, boldness to enter into the holiest by the blood of Jesus.

20 By a new and living way, which he hath consecrated for us, through the veil, that is to say, his flesh.

21 And having a high priest over the house of God;

22 Let us draw near with a true heart in full assurance of faith, having our hearts sprinkled from an evil conscience, and our bodies washed with pure water.

Jesus Christ's single sacrifice is completed by His unending position obtained from God's right hand. This gives believers a righteous access into the Sanctuary, the presence of God. It is for us to bond to the will power of God as having personal relationship with Him. Moreover He declared (John 14:6): *Jesus saith unto him, I am the way, the truth, and the life: no man cometh unto the Father, but by me.*

He is not of Himself but of His Father. He opened up the new and living way. He surrendered Himself by sacrificial offering on the Cross, apparently doing His Father's will. He was intimate with His Father while He surrendered His life for humanity. The call of God is besieging the saints to endeavour to do according to the will of God as you live a pleasing life to gain His approval. Genesis 1:3: *And God said, "Let there be light: and there was light.*

Faith is as you believing in the word, and action taken place with God's intervention. He is God, He is the word, and through the declaration of His words there are miracles in place. Hence, as He declared it, it came to pass because of the faith components. The element of faith is as God saw it and made a demand, hence you too can decree a thing and shall be established because you are the son/daughter of the living God.

All things were made by him; and without him was not anything made that was made.

Creation was by the Word of God: "And God said, Let there be light". According to

Roman 1:17: *For therein is the righteousness of God revealed from faith to faith: as it is written, THE JUST SHALL LIVE BY FAITH.*

Abiding in righteousness, God's essential attribute is revealed. It is not man's invention but God's revelation. What one believes does make a difference. He who believes that the gospel has life union while death is separation from God shall live by Faith.

1st John 5:4: *For whatsoever is born of God overcometh the world: and this is the victory that overcometh the world, even our faith.*

This is signposting to every born-again believer.

Galatians 3: 11: *But that no man is justified by the law in the sight of God, it is evident: for, THE JUST SHALL LIVE BY FAITH.*

He who is just because of his faith shall live forever.

As inscribed in the Bible for our knowledge and learning, Enoch did not see death. God took Enoch, He pleased God in doing His will and lived a life pleasing God. Saints, try to please God in all capacity doing His will that gives Him splendour in order to obtain His approval. Enoch was commended for his long wholesome life, and was a righteous man, the attitudes and character which pleased God are therefore worthy of consideration for believers to emulate.

Hebrew 11:5: *By faith Enoch was translated that he should not see death; AND WAS NOT FOUND, BECAUSE GOD HAD TRANSLATED HIM: for before his translation he had this testimony, that he pleased God.*

The expression pleased God as declared, (Genesis 5:22): *And Enoch walked with God after he begat Methuselah three hundred years, and begat sons and daughters*.

He walked with God. This godly man obviously allowed nothing to interrupt his personal relationship with God. He spoke the truth, as God revealed it to him. He went to heaven without dying; thus he had victory over death. He was a trustworthy vessel to whom God counted worthy. People of God, let us do His will and live pleasing lives unto Him. Age is no barrier, and whatever you are commanded to do for the sake of the Kingdom do not procrastinate. Saints, please make a demand from God to give you that courage, strength and grace that will enable you to obtain His approval. According to Genesis 6:9:

These are the generations of Noah: Noah was a just man and perfect in his generations, and Noah walked with God.

Noah was one of the ancient patriarchs who also was reckoned to be a righteous man. He was a just and perfect man during his era. Thus he did not conform or attach to moral standards but separated himself from the wickedness of his contemporaries and followed the Lord all the way through. The character of this godly man is instructive to every believer.

Hebrew 11:7: *By faith Noah, being warned of God of things not seen as yet, moved with fear, prepared an ark to the saving of his house; by which he condemned the world and became heir of the righteousness which is by faith.*

Noah was instructed by God to do in faith things that were incompatible with normality. He had never seen rain, yet when he was directed by God to build an ark because of a forthcoming flood, he obeyed by faith. He did not conform to the ungodliness that surrounded him but walked with God. Consequently, saints of God, please live a life that is pleasing unto God, and obedient to His callings. Noah had faith and believed in God. The significant feature of his faith was that he believed God, had confidence that God would keep His word; as He said it, surely it would come to pass. Such unquestioning obedience meets with God's approval. He attended to every detail of the construction of the ark, used only the materials that God commanded and was faithful. Noah would have been well informed of Enoch's prophecies of future judgement towards the ungodly (Jude 14-15):

14 And Enoch also, the seventh from Adam, prophesied of these, saying, Behold, the Lord cometh with ten thousand of his saints,

15 To execute judgment upon all, and to convince all that are ungodly among them of all their ungodly deeds which they have ungodly committed, and of all their hard speeches which ungodly sinners have spoken against him.

Hence, he too was called upon to speak of impending judgement, and that of an extraordinary nature which his contemporaries found hard to believe.

Some reckoned that the length of time between the giving of the warning and the flood was taking too long and it would never happen. During all that time, God waited, long sufferings. His faithful servant preached righteousness and the people never reacted to the warning, but ignored it.

1st Peter 3:19-20:

19 By which also he went and preached unto the spirits in prison;

20 Which sometime were disobedient, when once the longsuffering of God waited in the days of Noah, while the ark was a preparing, wherein few, that is, eight souls were saved by water.

The preaching was the announcement of Jesus' victory on the Cross of Calvary, which sealed the fate of those ruined souls. They heard and rejected Noah's preaching, and they were the largest group of humanity to experience the universal judgment of God. However, Jesus Christ descended into Hades, and He preached unto the spirits of those that had lost their souls in hell. Hence the quality of Noah's character pleased God. Saints, Noah was a human being with flesh and blood like you. If he can do this, those that believe in God can do the same to obtain His approval.

Matthew 24: 36-38:

36 *But of that day and hour knoweth no man, no, not the angels of heaven, but my Father only.*

37 *But as the days of Noah were, so shall also the coming of the Son of man be.*

38 *For as in the days that were before the flood they were eating and drinking, marrying and giving in marriage, until the day that Noah entered into the ark.*

This is a WAKE-UP CALL! Saints, as recorded, the days of Noah were pleasure-oriented and self-gratifying through marrying, celebrating, eating and drinking etc., thus carrying on the routine course of life without thinking of the impending judgment nor adhering to the warning of God through his servant. Let us be awake and do what is pleasing unto God, for tomorrow might be too late. The voice I knew you not shall not be ours Amen. Despite all odds with ungodly situations, and the indifferences, to his preaching, Noah was commended by God as being perfect. Can God boast about your deeds?

Furthermore, let us ponder on the account of Abraham. He was an idol worshipper in his home city of Ur. By faith he abandoned all that provides social security and even a sense of belonging, forwent all and sojourned in obedience unto an unknown destination. He did not question God (Genesis 12: 1-9):

1   *Now the Lord had said unto Abram, Get thee out of thy country, and from thy kindred, and from thy father's house, unto a land that I will show thee.*

2   *And I will make of thee a great nation, and I will bless thee and make thy name great; and thou shalt be a blessing:*

3   *And I will bless them that bless thee, and curse him that curseth thee: and in thee shall all families of the earth be blessed.*

4   *So Abram departed, as the LORD had spoken unto him; and Lot went with him; and Abram was seventy and five*

years old when he departed out of Haran.

5   *And Abram took Sarai his wife, and Lot his brother's son, and all their substance that they had gathered, and the souls that they had gotten in Haran; and they went forth to go into the land of Canaan; and into the land of Canaan they came.*

6   *And Abram passed through the land unto the place of Sichem, unto the plain of Moreh. And the Canaanite was then in the land.*

7   *And the LORD appeared unto Abram, and said, Unto thy seed will I give this land: and there builded he and altar unto the LORD, who appeared unto him.*

8   *And he removed from thence unto a mountain on the east of Beth-el, and pitched his tent, having Beth-el on the west, and Hai on the east: and there he builded an altar unto the LORD, and called upon the name of the LORD.*

9 And Abram journeyed, going on still toward the south.

God led Abram out of spiritual obscurity, so that through him all humanity might experience divine grace. He was called to leave his family and step out in faith. However, it was not an easy decision to separate from his people. As God called Abram out, He was still sending forth disciples for the great commission. Are you ready to step out in faith? People of God, you cannot witness for Christ, if you perceive what people will say or hold against you, or due to your educational background, even your family history, or whatever reason because of irrelevant excuses, no matter what the circumstances, you have no excuse.

Abraham never asked God where or what destination. He wasn't from a Christian background and was an idol worshipper. Or was there no one God could send? But Abraham was so faithful and obeyed while he was tested in various dimensions. He lived a life that delighted God, doing His will. As an act of hospitality he entertained angels unaware, while they later pronounced a promised of God blessing unto him and Sarai, gift of a son.

Genesis: 18:1-15: However, without faith you cannot obey His commandment neither able to hear nor listen to His voice. He was a man of faith, obedient servant. God respected him and granted him his approval.

Saints, you never know when you entertain angels of God. Hence the Parable of the Good Samaritan was narrated. A certain lawyer was having a discussion with Jesus Christ and was willing to justify himself. In response Jesus said, as long as you do good to the least of your brothers, it is counted as doing God's will (Luke 10: 25-37). Jesus Christ's demonstration of Love as He does is without any bias. Many people are keen to help people from whom they can obtain accolades or honour. Not so with the Kingdom Principles for pleasing God. Abraham never expected he would be entertaining a guest. However, because it was his routine lifestyle, that drastically changed his story and granted him a long-awaited promise.

Furthermore, Abraham's faith was being tested but believed that God can provide a substitute for his son Isaac (Genesis 22:1-19). The full story of his encounter with the angels of God from Verses: 11-12:

11   And the angel of the LORD called unto him out of heaven, and said, Abraham, Abraham: and he said, Here am I.

12   And he said, Lay not thine hand upon the lad, neither do thou anything unto him: for now I know that thou fearest God, seeing thou hast not withheld thy son, thine only son from me.

This was the entire purpose of the Moriah. He obtained approval after being tested and God acknowledged that Abraham feared Him. God made an alternative provision of a ram as a substitute for Isaac. Therefore those who followed Jesus by faith (Hebrew 10:35-39) place their feet on a marked path.

Additionally he obtained approval when Abraham interceded on behalf of a nation (Sodom) (Genesis 18:22-33). The question is, who are the nation? They were people with flesh and blood, the handiwork of God. Many people do not care about others due to self-interest. The Lord is telling you to rise up and bring our nation back to God in prayers (interceding), because without faith no one can please God. Wherever you are in the world, you need to intercede and take our nation back to God. Let us be awake, strive to do His will and live a life that is pleasing unto Him for approval. Believers are the spiritual seed of Abraham, the forefather of both the Jews and the Arabs (Genesis 12:1-3):

1   *Now the LORD had said unto Abram, Get thee out of thy country, and from thy kindred, and from thy father's house, unto a land that I will show thee:*

2   *And I will make of thee a great nation, and I will bless thee and make thy name great; and thou shalt be a blessing:*

3   *And I will bless them that bless thee, and curse him that curseth thee: and in thee shall all families of the earth be blessed.*

Even Abraham's servant emulates his master in faith as he worshipped God, able to accomplish the errand of his master (Genesis 24:52)

And it came to pass, that when Abraham's servant heard their words, he worshipped the LORD, bowing himself to the earth.

Abraham's servant fetched Isaac a wife (Rebecca) after praying for a sign to signify the chosen bride as pre-planned by God and as directed by his master. Can people emulate your lifestyle? Are you the epitome of good deeds? I could reflect back on some part of the world where masters/mistresses maltreat their maids and manservants. They never realised those involved are just victims of circumstances doing odd jobs to earn a living. My suggestion is, whoever is within your reach please do not withdraw help, because they are your neighbours. Consequently, there are some documented examples of people such as Jephthah in faith; he was a son of a harlot but conquered many cities. He was an outcast but was later selected, and became a sought-after man who delivered his nation (Israel).

Judges 11: 1-11:

1   *Now Jephthah the Gileadite was a mighty man of valour and he was the son of a harlot: and Gilead begat Jephthah.*

2   *And Gilead's wife bare him sons; and his wife's sons grew up, and they thrust out Jephthah, and said unto him, Thou shalt not inherit in our father's house; for thou art the son of a strange woman.*

3   *Then Jephthah fled from his brethren, and dwelt in the land of Tob: and there were gathered vain men to Jephthah, and went out with him.*

4   *And it came to pass in process of time, that the children of Ammon made war against Israel.*

5   *And it was so, that when the children of Ammon made war against Israel, the elders of Gilead went to fetch Jephthah out of the land of Tob:*

6   *And they said unto Jephthah, Come, and be our captain, that we may fight with the children of Ammon.*

7   *And Jephthah said unto the elders of Gilead, Did not ye hate me, and expel me out of my father's house? And why are ye come unto me now when ye are in distress?*

8   *And the elders of Gilead said unto Jephthah, Therefore we turn again to thee now, that thou mayest go with us, and fight against the children of Ammon, and be our head over all the inhabitants of Gilead.*

9   And Jephthah said unto the elders of Gilead, If ye bring me home again to fight against the children of Ammon, and the LORD deliver them before me, shall I be your head?

10 And the elders of Gilead said unto Jephthah, The LORD be witness between us, if we do not so according to thy words.

11 Then Jephthah went with the elders of Gilead, and the people made him head and Captain over them: and Jephthah uttered all his words before the LORD in Mizpeh.

Jephthah was one of the Judges of Israel, the illegitimate son of Gilead, and was called to be the captain of the forces and deliverer of the people who had rejected him. Saints of God, where have you being rejected? I will advise you to keep doing what seems good for pleasing God, loving and caring in accordance to the scripture. It will not be too long before the Lord will remember you, as when He opened the book of remembrance to Mordecai (Esther 6:1-3):

1   On that night could not the king sleep, and he commanded to bring the book of records of the chronicles; and they were read before the king.

2   And it was found written, that Mordecai had told of Bigthana and Teresh, two of the king's chamberlains, the keepers of the door, who sought to lay hand on the king Ahasuerus.

3   And the king said, What honour and dignity hath been done to Mordecai for this? Then said the king's servants that ministered unto him, There is nothing done for him.

Be assured that even though people may have forgotten you, you should keep doing His will and have a positive attitude towards your fellow beings. God is a rewarder. He will never forget your labour of love, and you shall be accepted at the end. Mordecai was not paying lip service but diligently doing his job in fear of God. Later, at the appointed period the Lord remembered him with honour and dignified him forcefully in the presence of his adversary (Haman). There are accounts of men and women of faith as recorded like Rahab (Hebrew 11:31-32):

*31 By faith the harlot Rahab perished not
with them that believed not, when she
had received the spies with peace.*

*32 And what shall I more say? For the time
would fail me to tell of Gideon, and of
Barak, and of Samson, and of
Jephthah; of David also, and Samuel,
and of the prophets:*

Rahab was a woman of faith as God is with the
children of Israel. She feared God as she hid the
two spies in her house with peace, because she
believed that God of Israel was the true God and
her faith was commended. Her demonstration of
faith by good works was registered and the fall of
Jericho followed. Rahab was spared with her
household. Afterwards, she gave birth to a son,
Boaz, who got married to Ruth and became the
father of Obed (Ruth 4:20-22):

*20 And Amminadah begat Nahshon, and
Nahshon begat Salmon,*

*21 And Salmon begat Boaz, and Boaz begat
Obed,*

*22 And Obed begat Jesse, and Jesse begat
David.*

Thereafter, a Canaanite harlot became part of the lineage of King David, from whom the Messiah descended.

As mentioned above, although they went through trials and passed their tests, they recovered their honour instead of shame, and became celebrities. Jephthah became captain over his people. Rahab, Jephthah, or anyone else must have been labelled, but they became a solution to their generation. Instead of shame they became famous and impacted their world, which became a city that can never be forsaken.

Saints, where have you being rejected? Are you still dwelling on your past, seeking someone's approval, and who will grant you the go-ahead to do what God had laid into your heart to fulfil your destiny? The only way forward is to have faith in Him, live a life that is pleasing unto God, doing His will, then you shall obtain His signature. Although you might be thinking that no one remembers or sees what you are doing, rest assured that someday where you have been overlooked, Jehovah, who remembered Joseph, will send His ministry angels to present your case. You have to do your bit, but God will definitely manifest in your affairs. We should not be carried away with the challenges of this world. Trust and have faith in Him, He will show up on your behalf. If there is any ugly situation in your life, it shall be eradicated by the power in the Blood of Jesus Christ Amen.

Can we reflect on the book of Daniel? In regard to the three Hebrew young men who were sojourners, they never compromised towards materialism (Daniel 3:16-18):

16 Shadrach, Meshach and Abednego, answered and said to the King, O Nebuchadnezzar, we are not careful to answer thee in this matter.

17 If it be so, our God whom we serve is able to deliver us from the burning fiery furnace, and he will deliver us out of thine, hand, O king.

18 But if not, be it known unto thee, O king, that we will not serve thy gods, nor worship the golden image which thou hast set up.

Daniel was represented as a specifically dedicated and humble man who feared God, and he and his friends walked with God. There was no sign of any lapse of faith in them as they believed God even when they were thrown into a furnace. They held on to their faith, that if it pleased God to preserve and deliver them, He would. They were not moved, but only believed God's will should be done they were heavenly bound, hence they could not deny their faith.

What can we learn from this trial? The fire of fury was burning as they were cast into it. Will you compromise because of what you will eat and drink, the payment of bills? There was a dispute about wearing the Cross on official duty, but the woman involved held unto her faith whilst she defended it. Saints, it is time for us to practise what we believe. We should always look up and be aware that somebody is watching all we are doing, whether it is good nor bad. I will submit that we rather do the will of God and live life pleasing unto Him to be accepted.

Chapter Three

OBEDIENCE

———⬦—⬦———

This is a concept which holds for both the Old Testament and the New Testament. Obedience expresses an action which can exist in ordinary associations such as servants to their masters or children to their parents. Its significant reference is to a relationship that should exist between man and God (Pfeiffer et al., 2000). God reveals Himself to man through His voice and words. Words are envisioned to be heard. This obviously involves a physical reception of the words with a recognised mental apprehension of their meaning.

But in terms of man's reception of God's revelation, this in itself is not true hearing. True hearing is faith which receives the divine Word and translates it into action. It is a faith response. To hear is to act. In other words, to really hear God's Word is to obey God's Word. With the revelation John had received on Patmos (Revelation 1:3):

Blessed is he that readeth, and they that hear the words of this prophecy, and keep those things which are written therein: for the time is at hand.

Therefore, there is supposed to be no contradiction between hearing and obedience. True hearing is obedience. Faith itself involves obedience, and Jesus, Paul and James make it quite clear that true faith issues is obedience (Pfeiffer et al., 2000). According to Romans 5:19:

For as by one man's disobedience many were made sinners, so by the obedience of one shall man be made righteous.

The Epistle of Paul was illustrating the fact that the Adamic nature brought sins which individuals committed led to the reign of death. Now, as people respond in faith and accept the gift of life offered by Christ, the quality of righteousness will be expressed in their actions as it was recorded in the transforming grace of God. Even so, according to 1st Peter 1:2:

Elect according to the foreknowledge of God the Father, through sanctification of the Spirit, unto obedience and sprinkling of the blood of Jesus Christ: Grace unto you, and peace, be multiplied.

Those are the chosen of God unto salvation. It is not simple prescience of advance knowledge. It is God's determination in eternity past to bring some people into a distinct relationship with Himself. The Spirit sets apart for salvation from destruction those whom God had foreknown.

Hence (Exodus 24:1-11):

1 **And he said unto Mosses, Come up unto the LORD, thou, and Aaron, Nadab, and Abihu, and seventy of the elders of Israel; and worship ye afar off.**

2 **And Moses alone shall come near the LORD: but they shall not come nigh; neither shall the people go up with him.**

3 **And Moses came and told the people all the words of the LORD, and all the judgments: and all the people answered**

*with one voice, and said, All the words
which the LORD hath said will we do.*

4   *And Moses wrote all the words of the
LORD, and rose up early in the
morning, and builded an altar under
the hill, and twelve pillars, according to
the twelve tribes of Israel.*

5   *And he sent young men of the children
of Israel, which offered burnt offerings,
and sacrificed peace offerings of oxen
unto the LORD.*

6   *And Moses took half of the blood, and
put it in basins; and half of the blood he
sprinkled on the altar.*

7   *And he took the book of the covenant,
and read in the audience of the people:
and they said that the LORD hath said
will we do, and be obedient.*

8   *And Moses took the blood, and sprinkled
it on the people, and said, Behold the
blood of the covenant, which the LORD
hath made with you concerning all
these words.*

9   *Then went up Moses, and Aaron, Nadab, and Abihu, and seventy of the elders of Israel:*

10   *And they saw the God of Israel: and there was under his feet as it were a paved work of a sapphire stone, and as it were the body of heaven in his clearness.*

11   *And upon the nobles of the children of Israel he laid not his hand: also they saw God, and did eat and drink.*

The blood of the covenant is the expression from which the Old Testament gets originality. Hence God's demonstrations of His sovereignty towards mankind but with the obedience of a leader chosen to execute His purposes. The whole life of the Israelites was administered by God, politically, socially, economically and spiritually.

What about the Commandment as directed through God to Moses (Exodus 20:1-17):

1   *And God spake all these words, saying,*

2   *I am the LORD thy God, which have brought thee out of the land of Egypt, out of the house of bondage.*

3   *Thou shalt have no other gods before me.*

4   *Thou shalt not make unto thee any graven image, or any likeness of anything that is in heaven above, or that is in the earth beneath, or that is in the water under the earth:*

5   *Thou shalt not bow down thyself to them, nor serve them: for I the LORD thy God am a jealous God, visiting the iniquity of the fathers upon the children unto the third and fourth generation of them that hate me;*

6   *And showing mercy unto thousands of them that love me, and keep my commandments.*

7   *Thou shalt not take the name of the LORD thy God in vain: for the LORD will not hold him guiltless that taketh his name in vain.*

8   *Remember the Sabbath day, to keep it holy.*

9   *Six days shalt thou labour, and do all thy work:*

10   *But the seventh day is the Sabbath of the LORD thy God: in it thou shalt not*

do any work, thou, nor thy son, nor thy daughter, thy manservant, nor thy maidservant, nor thy cattle, nor thy stranger that is within thy gates:

11 *For in six days the LORD made heaven and earth, the seas and all that in them is, and rested the seventh day: wherefore the LORD blessed the Sabbath day, and hallowed it.*

12 *Honour thy father and thy mother: that thy days may be long upon the land which the LORD thy God giveth thee:*

13 *Thou shalt not kill.*

14 *Thou shalt not commit adultery.*

15 *Thou shalt not steal.*

16 *Thou shalt not bear false witness against thy neighbour.*

17 *Thou shalt not covet thy neighbour's house, thou shalt not covet thy neighbour's wife, nor his manservant, nor his maidservant, nor his ox, nor his ass, nor any thing that is thy neighbour's.*

The commandment teaches that no deity, nor any thing you give priority before God, should be regarded as a god that you adored. The Almighty God only should be the priority, the one to serve and always first in all your endeavours. Our character, attitudes, how we relate to our brethren, in the workplace, family, gathering anywhere you might find yourselves. He has no rival but the only true God. The verses demand the demonstrations of an exclusive covenant relationship with God and to humanity (Psalms 81 9: 10)

There shall no strange god be in thee, neither shalt thou worship any strange god.

I am the LORD thy God, which brought thee out of the land of Egypt: open thy mouth wide and I will fill it.

God is jealous and was referring to the miraculous deliverance: therefore, His people should believe and trust Him only and obey His commandment and do His will to be accepted. The above verses are embedded in the Commandment of Jesus the last and the greatest (Mark 12:28-31):

28 And one the scribes came and having heard them reasoning together, and perceiving that he had answered them well, asked him, Which is the first commandment of all?

29 *And Jesus answered him, The first of all the commandment is HEAR, O ISRAEL; THE LORD OUR GOD IS ONE LORD:*

30 *AND THOU SHALT LOVE THE LORD THY GOD WITH ALL THY HEART, AND WITH ALL THY SOUL, AND WITH ALL THY MIND, AND WITH ALL THY STRENGTH: this is the first commandment.*

31 *And the second is like, namely this, THOU SHALT LOVE THY NEIGHBOR AS THYSELF. There is none other commandment greater than these.*

Therefore saints, if we fear and love, you will not perceive, nor venture to do evil, nor betray, nor harm your fellow human being. It's embedded in daily living, either within the spiritual or secular domain.

Additionally, in obedience Moses was able to execute the types of Tabernacle as constructively instructed by God (Exodus 26). The complicated design of the Tabernacle teaches believers about the scriptural doctrine of sacrificial atonement that entails personal consecration intended to help us understand how we are to approach God through worship. Hence, the sacrificial offering of Jesus Christ on Calvary interceding on our behalf. Such detailed structure with designated materials is so spiritually significant to the people of God at this time of life. Apostle Paul confidently speaks of himself as a wise master builder who laid the one and only foundation which is in Jesus Christ (1st Corinthians 3:9-13):

9　*For we are labourers together with God: ye are God's husbandry, ye are God's building.*

10　*According to the grace of God which is given unto me, as a wise master builder, I have laid the foundation, and another buildeth thereon. But let everyman take heed how he buildeth there upon.*

11　*For other foundation can no man lay than that is laid, which is Jesus Christ.*

12　*Now if any man build upon this foundation gold, silver; precious stones, wood, hay, stumble;*

13 Every man's work shall be made manifest: for the day shall declare it, because it shall be revealed by fire; and the fire shall try every man's work of what sort it is.

Moses was a servant of God; he was a man like you. If he could obey, to do His will as commanded, why can't you and I hearken to His commandment too? The above passages emphasise that believers are labourers together with God, thus we are co-labourers. Do the work of God without paying lip service, because God is the only one that will test your obedience. Your right standing with Him, attitude, character, living a righteous living. Saints, we should realise that our body is the temple of the Most High God; our quota can draw men unto Christ or send them away. Can this question be asked: are our lifestyles evangelising Christ or not? Let's bear in mind that every man's work shall be made apparent, and be revealed by fire. Therefore, in what category will yours be classified? If in doubt, I implore you to strive to build towards the Kingdom of Heaven that will enable you and me to obtain acceptance before God.

Although Israel failed to keep this provisional covenant because of their sinful acts, God promised through Jeremiah's prophecy the establishment of an unconditional Covenant of Grace which is the news that believers are enjoying (Jeremiah 31:31-34):

31 Behold, the days come, saith the LORD, that I will make a new covenant with the house of Israel, and with the house of Judah.

32 Not according to the covenant that I made with their fathers in the day that I took them by the hand to bring them out of the land of Egypt; which my covenant they brake, although I was a husband unto them, saith the LORD:

33 But this shall be the covenant that I will make with the house of Israel; After those days, saith the LORD, I will put my law in their inward parts, and write it in their hearts; and will be their God, and they shall be my people.

34 And they shall teach no more every man his neighbour, and every man his

brother, saying, Know the LORD: for
they shall all know me, from the least of
them unto the greatest of them, saith the
LORD: for I will forgive their iniquity,
and I will remember their sin no more.

Jeremiah foretells in the New Testament that God will extend His hand of grace to the Gentiles. From this new covenant, God will call out people for Himself from all the nations of the world towards the bride of Christ (Revelation 21:1-9). Therefore, this news (the sinless Christ) and the unconditional Covenant is much greater than the Old Covenant because it rests on the ability of Jesus Christ's atonement for the universe.

Jesus was the Son of God: He obeyed His father (Hebrew 5:8): *Though he were a Son, yet learned he obedience by the things which he suffered.*

Although He was the Son of the Living God, in obedience he hearkened to the voice of His Father because He had compassion, perhaps because it was pre-planned that he would be crucified on the Cross of Calvary for the world. He obeyed and declared not of His own but the will of His Father that he needed to endure the Gethsemane ordeal.

He sacrificed himself as a perfect offering for the sinful world and was accepted as He pleases God for approval. Saints, what are you and I going through? Jesus our model suffered for the sake of the kingdom. He has been through whatever challenge you are experiencing.

Hence, from the Gethsemane ordeal (Mark 14: 32-42):

32 *And they came to a place which was named Gethsemane: and he saith to his disciples, Sit ye here, while I shall pray.*

33 *And he taketh with him Peter and James and John, and began to be sore amazed, and to be very heavy;*

34 *And saith unto them, My soul is exceeding sorrowful unto death: tarry ye here, and watch.*

35 *And he went forward a little, and fell on the ground, and prayed that, if it were possible, the hour might pass from him.*

36 *And he said, Abba, Father, all things are possible unto thee; take away this cup from me; nevertheless not what I will, but what thou wilt.*

37 And he cometh, and findeth them sleeping, and saith unto Peter, Simon, sleepest thou? Couldest not thou watch one hour?

38 Watch ye and pray, lest ye enter into temptation. The spirit truly is ready, but the flesh is weak.

39 And again he went away, and prayed, and spake the same words.

40 And when he returned, he found them asleep again, (for their eyes were heavy,) neither wist they what to answer him.

41 And he cometh the third time, and saith unto them, Sleep on now, and take your rest: it is enough, the hour is come; behold, the Son of man is betrayed into the hands of sinners.

42 Rise up, let us go; lo, he that betrayeth me is at hand.

It could be referred to as the wilderness experience. From the last two verses Apostle Peter vividly *denied Jesus* as predicted by Jesus Christ. Beloved saints, when faced with trial or going through the challenges of life, never minding is part of the Christian journey. There are men/women documented in the Scripture as they went through trial, test of faith, even Our Master Jesus went through it and came out triumphantly. As a believer, it is just for a moment; it will not be long that you and I shall testify to the goodness of God. Nevertheless, at various instances while going through issues of life, that particular period you are on you own.

The rationale behind it is that the journey is a personal race, which is experiential. I suggest you should not give up, and do not throw in the towel too soon. At the end of the race there is only you and your creator. All our patriarch forefathers went through it, and they were accepted and respected by God. You and I shall have victory in whatever challenges we might be going through. Just have faith in Him, trust that He is able to do exceedingly and abundantly above all we could imagine. *Jesus Christ the same yesterday, and today, and forever* (Hebrew 13: 8).

Most believers are unable to take that bold step of faith to "forge ahead", as delayed obedience might result in delayed blessing. Divine blessing is from obeying the commandment of God. What has He demanded of you to do for the Kingdom; hence that would lead towards your fulfillment? Your place of fulfilment is an act of obedience, your place of *"there"*. In obedience Elijah was commanded by God to migrate from the brook Cherith behind Jordan and be relocated to the widow of Zarephath without hesitation:

1st Kings 17: 8-16:

8   *And the word of the LORD came unto him, saying,*

9   *Arise, get thee to Zarephath, which belongeth to Zidon, and dwell there: behold, I have commanded a widow woman there to sustain thee.*

10 *So he arose and went to Zarephath. And when he came to the gate of the city, behold, the widow woman was there gathering of sticks: and he called to her, and said, Fetch me, I pray thee, a little water in a vessel, that I may drink.*

11 *And as she was going to fetch it, he called to her, and said, Bring me, I pray thee, a morsel of bread in thine hand.*

12 *And she said, As the LORD thy God*

liveth, I have not a cake, but a handful of meal in a barrel, and a little oil in a cruse: and, behold, I am gathering two sticks, that I may go in and dress it for me and my son, that we may eat it, and die.

13 *And Elijah said unto her, Fear not; go and do as thou hast said: but make me thereof a little cake first, and bring it unto me, and after make for thee and for thy son.*

14 *For thus saith the LORD God of Israel, The barrel of meal shall not waste, neither shall the cruse of oil fail, until the day that the LORD sendeth rain upon the earth.*

15 *And she went and did according to the saying of Elijah: and she, and he, and her house, did eat many days.*

16 *And the barrel of meal wasted not, neither did the cruse of oil fail, according to the word of the LORD, which he spake by Elijah.*

In obedience Elijah was sustained throughout the three-year famine, as he was fed by the raven before relocating to the widow. The prophet was obedient, while the woman was also obedient to the reassurance of the voice of the man of God. The Lord cared for Elijah, so also the widow. The woman was able to care for her family and the man of God. Her life was transformed by entertaining the servant of God. The same is applicable to saints of God when we listened to the voice of the Lord, doing His will, able to live a godly living, pleasing God and able to lift other people's burdens, loving one another as oneself.

Beloved, whatever HE asked you to do please do it (John 2:5). Mary the mother of Jesus advised His disciples to adhere to the commandment of Jesus. Although you might be thinking, what would people say? Who will reaffirm your action? Where will the funding come from? Rest assured that if the Lord has really called you out for His divine assignment, *Jehovah Jireh* (The great Provider will show Himself powerfully). Nonetheless, before the Lord does anything, He will watch your motives and your character/attitude. He will back you up when you take that action in obedience according to His will.

In the book of Joshua God reaffirmed him that he should "be courageous" and "fear not".

In most instances believers are gripped with fear, but definitely He will understand your circumstances. Do you realise that whatever you have been through is working together for the goodness of God, and you don't need to be dismayed? There are people out there awaiting your testimony, awaiting your input at the local or international level for you to change your world. If God laid anything into your heart without doing it, if anything happens, and you passed unto glory, the Lord will make a demand from you. We shall not be condemned. I implored you to be awake and take your place to impact your world, for heaven and hell are real.

However, in Joseph's account (Genesis 37:7) he stated:

For behold we were binding sheaves in the field, and, lo, my sheaves arose, and also stood upright; and, behold, your sheaves stood round about, and made obeisance to my sheaf.

This was about Joseph's dream that threw him from prison and lately to Palace.

The ordeal of Joseph was when he revealed his

dreams to his brethren, which suggested the family would one day "bow down" to honour him. His brothers plotted to murder him but he was rescued by the eldest (Reuben), and finally his dream came to pass, while the family bowed for obeisance. Although, before the fulfilment, he went through captivity, and was imprisoned due to Potiphar's wife (Genesis 39: 2-4 and 9):

2 And the LORD was with Joseph, and he was a prosperous man; and he was in the house of his master the Egyptian.

3 And his master saw that the LORD was with him, and that the LORD made all that he did to prosper in his hand.

4 And Joseph found grace in his sight; and he served him: and he made him overseer over his house, and all that he had he put unto his hand.

9 There is none greater in this house than I; neither hath he kept back anything from me but thee; because thou are his wife: how then can I do this great wickedness; and sin against God?

God made Joseph prosperous. He refused to

compromise and was obedient to his master and unto God. However, at the set time with the agenda of God he ended up in the palace. Wherever we have been hated and of no relevance, God will make you and me rulers over the enemies of our destiny.

Joseph was a child that obtained favour from God and from man. He feared God and chose to obey Him. He suffered for it, but God gave him a reward at the end. It is for our warning and learning that God reigns in the affairs of His people. Joseph would have chosen to betray his master because of temporary enjoyment that would have demoralized his destiny, but instead in obedience and in fear of the Lord he lived a lifestyle that pleased God and earned him a certificate of approval at the end. Saints, we can do likewise. Whatever position you might be in, you are the Bible people are reading.

Chapter Four

GIVING/OFFERING

It was accredited to Job as a righteous and just man with good works towards his families and friends (Job 42:7-10):

7 **And it was so, that after the LORD had spoken these words unto Job, the LORD said to Eliphaz the Temanite, My wrath is kindled against thee, and against thy two friends: for ye have not spoken of me the thing that is right, as my servant Job hath.**

8   *Therefore take unto you now seven bullocks and seven rams, and go to my servant Job, and offer up for yourselves a burnt offering; and my servant Job shall pray for you: for him will I accept: lest I deal with you after your folly, in that ye have not spoken of me the thing which is right, like my servant Job.*

9   *So Eliphaz the Temanite and Bildad the Shuhite and Zophar the Naamathite went, and did according as the LORD commanded them: the LORD also accepted Job.*

10 *And the Lord turned the captivity of Job, when he prayed for his friends: also the LORD gave Job twice as much as he had before.*

The previous verse was when Job submitted to God's will and authority. From the demonstration for us, we must let God's perfect love cast out our fear but trust solely in the Lord and abandon reliance on any righteousness of ours, although Job's friends were rebuked for their faults, while Eliphaz was singled out as the leader of the three friends. Nevertheless, the Lord referred to Job as

His servant in four instances from Job 42 verses 7-8 for his acceptance of God's approval.

This is food for thought, that we might wrong God if we fall into the way of thinking of Job's three friends. We wrong Him if each trial is excused by condemning ourselves for supposed sins. Instead, we need to approach God with trust in His love and His righteousness. His purposes will be for our good. God assures those who suffer for doing the right thing that, when such suffering comes, it is for a special purposeful, planned act of the Lord for good. Though Christ also suffered, He was innocent, and through that suffering, He accomplished the wonderful purpose of bringing humanity to God (1st Peter 3:13-18).

On diverse occasions, we may not know why we are faced or sometimes go through a challenge in life. Saints, we can know that the suffering of God's peculiar people is purposive and envisioned for good. The scenario was similar to the account of Jesus, but the issue is for the saints to hold unto God when trials or challenges show up; we just need to trust Him.

During Jesus Christ's mission on earth, the human race that He did good for with all sort of miracles, signs and wonders hailed Him with applause and chanted Hosanna. At the end, they turned against Him to nail Him on the Cross by chanting 'Crucify Him'. It was a pre-planned agenda of God, but the devil executed an evil plot through Judas Iscariot.

The rationale of this focus was apparently the act of giving. Job was able to give his time and resources before the misfortune but still endeavoured to pray for his friends despite all the trials he was going through. Nevertheless, he was being mocked by friends when going through trials , but God reassured Eliphaz (Job's friend) in verses 7b-8 while He also referred to Job as His servant on four occasions in the above verses.

With the commendation of God, Job was able to be accepted and gained the certificate of approval. Why was that? Jehovah sees your intention. What you and I are thinking towards one another means a lot to Him, your perception, character and attitude towards one another. No wonder! The offering of Cain was not accepted, while Abel's was accepted (Genesis 4: 3-7):

3   And in process of time it came to pass, that Cain brought of the fruit of the ground an offering unto the LORD.

4   *And Abel, he also brought of the
     firstlings of his flock and of the fat
     thereof, And the LORD had respect unto
     Abel and to his offering.*

5   *But unto Cain and to his offering he
     had not respect. And Cain was very
     wroth, and his countenance fell.*

6   *And the LORD said unto Cain, Why art
     thou wroth?, and why is thy
     countenance fallen?*

7   *If thou doest well, shalt thou not be
     accepted? And if thou doest not well, sin
     lieth at the door. And unto thee shall be
     his desire, and thou shalt rule over him.*

From the above scripture it is obvious that from the entire account Abel's offering was more excellent because it was the right kind of offering, as well as being made with the right attitude (Hebrew 11:4):

By faith Abel offered unto God a more excellent sacrifice than Cain, by which he obtained witness that he was righteous, God testifying of his gifts: and by it he being dead yet speaketh.

On that account, with positive motives by faith Abel's sacrifice was "better".

The principle of sacrifice had been demonstrated to Adam and Eve in their clothing, which was made from the skins of animals. Only Abel brought lambs, while Cain brought farm products. It may have been the best he had, because redemption knows no other acceptable sacrifice but "blood". Cain's anger had already been demonstrated by a negative approach that resulted in him murdering his brother Abel. His underlying attitude towards God was shown by his reaction because he was very wrathful. Nonetheless, God's gentle advices still left Cain unharmed (Gen. 4:6-7).

Conversely, that was the start of a lengthy account of mortal violence and man's inhumanity towards his fellow men. No wonder. If love had not been wanting, Cain would not have murdered his brother. God is still in the business of caring. If you love you would not kill nor steal nor do evil to your fellow human being. You cannot obtain approval from God if you are callous or wicked to your brethren.

We read about Tabitha whom Peter raised from the dead due to her good work (Act 9: 36-43):

36 *Now there was at Joppa a certain disciple named Tabitha, which by interpretation is called Dorcas: this woman was full of good works and almsdeeds which she did.*

37 *And it came to pass in those days, that she was sick, and died: whom when they had washed, they laid her in an upper chamber.*

38 *And forasmuch as Lydda was nigh to Joppa, and the disciples had heard that Peter was there, they sent unto him two men, desiring him that he would not delay to come to them.*

39 *Then Peter arose and went with them, when he was come, they brought him into the upper chamber; and all the widows stood by him weeping and showing the coats and garments which Dorcas made; while she was with them.*

40 *But Peter put them all forth, and kneeled down, and prayed; and turning him to the body said, Tabitha, arise. And she opened her eyes: and when she saw Peter, she sat up.*

41 *And he gave her his hand, and lifted her up, and when he had called the saints and widows, presented her alive.*

42 *And it was known throughout all Joppa; and many believed in the Lord.*

43 *And it came to pass, that he tarried many days in Joppa with one Simon, a tanner.*

Saints, what would people say about you when you are not around? That little gift of God in you is enough to impact your world.

Tabitha was one of the disciples of Christ, and not only that; but was eminent above many, for works of charity. She made a business of doing good and having learned to maintain good works (Titus 3: 8):

"She was a good doer as a tree that is full of fruit. Many are full of good words, who are empty and barren in good works; but Tabitha was a great doer, not great talker: Non magna loquimur, sed vivimus - We do not talk great things, but we live them" (Henry's Commentary, 2000).

This disciple of Christ performed many alms deeds, also work of charity and generosity, gracefully caring for her fellow citizens and being a blessing to humanity. This is the lifestyle and character of a good steward, which all the disciple of Christ should imitate. As inscribed according to the scripture that is promised to those who consider the poor; not that they shall never be sick, but Almighty God will strengthen them even when they are in pain during sickness (Psalm 41: 1, 3):

1   Blessed is the he that considereth the poor: the LORD will deliver him in time of trouble.

3   The LORD will strengthen him upon the bed of languishing: thou wilt make all his bed in his sickness.

What will you and I be remembered for?

King David reaffirmed that he would not give mere gifts to God. He acknowledged a sacrificial offering.

2nd Samuel 24: 21, 24-25:

21 And Araunah said, Wherefore is my lord the king come to his servant? And David said, To buy the threshing floor of thee, to build an altar unto the LORD, that the plague may be stayed from the people.

24 And the King said unto Araunah, Nay, but I will surely buy it of thee at a price neither will I offer burnt offerings unto the LORD my God of that which doth cost me nothing. So David bought the threshing floor and the oxen for fifty shekels of silver.

25 And David built there an altar unto the LORD, and offered burnt offerings and peace offerings, So the LORD was entreated for the land, and the plague was stayed from Israel.

The apparent incongruity between the fifty shekels paid to Araunah mentioned and the amount of six hundred recorded by the writer of 1st Chronicles 21:24 perhaps has to do with the differences in the amount of land purchased as indicated in the two accounts. The book of Samuel describes the threshing floor as a designated site for the house of God, while the book of Chronicles stated that the whole territory including the threshing floor was very expensive. Hence, the bigger location was for Solomon's temple, thus for the Lord's Sanctuary. Nevertheless, the book of Samuel was concerned about the sacrificial offerings that necessitated the staying of the plague in Verses 21, 25. Similarly the below verses was in conjunction with the above Scripture:

King David said to Ornan, Nay; but I will verily buy it for the full price: for I will not take that which is thine for the LORD, nor offer burnt offerings without cost (1st Chronicle 21:24).

The above references signify how King David feared God and was able to give sacrificially thereby stopping the plague. The land embraced change and there was peace in the land. When you have exhausted all your efforts with fasting and prayers, and all attempts to get positive results are to no avail, then to move your request to the next level you should give an offering, by sowing sacrificially. This is an act of passion and love of God that will prompt you to release your substance to honour God. Giving is mandatory and is a command for us to be blessed. The sacrificial offering can break any siege (2nd Samuel 24: 24-25).

Some believers find it very difficult to give an offering to worship God during services. They rather gather coins that are not needed in their homes for the House of God. For your information, saints, whatever you have that cannot be utilised to meet your need or purpose, you don't have to offer such a gift as an offering unto God. Jesus Christ was among the congregation while He was watching that widow with her last two mites (Luke: 21: 1-4):

1   *And he looked up, and saw the rich men casting their gift into the treasure.*

2   *And he saw also a certain poor widow casting in thither two mites.*

3   *And he said, Of a truth I say unto you, that this poor widow hath cast in more than they all:*

4   *For all these have of their abundance cast in unto the offerings of God: but she of her penury hath cast in all the living that she had.*

Jesus was able to view the attitudes of all the congregation towards the offering. People who had banknotes, instead of preparing their offering at home, lifted the envelope, signalling that it was not loose coins but notes. We should know that our gift is not to intimidate nor oppress the poor, but between you and your creator. God is watching your heart of thanksgiving in honour to Him; this was the message he was trying to relate to people here. You are giving to God, not unto man. This widow brought all that she had; God saw that it was brought out of passion, thus the motives behind giving towards the kingdom.

Beloved of God, we should realise that tithes and offerings are a commandment from God for the wellbeing of His people (Malachi 3: 8-10):

8   *Will a man rob God? Yet ye have robbed me. But ye say, wherein have we robbed thee? In tithes and offerings.*

9   *Ye are cursed with a curse for ye have robbed me, even this whole nation.*

10   *Bring ye all the tithes into the storehouse, that there may be meat in mine house, and prove me now herewith, saith the Lord of hosts, if I will not open you the windows of heaven, and pour you out a blessing, that there shall not be room enough to receive it.*

Tithing is mandatory as commanded by God. It is the practice of giving 10 percent of one's income to the Lord. It is called "storehouse tithing" thus:

the tithe be given to the Lord through the local church, because that is where you are being nurtured or fed with the word of God. However, the money or resources are meant to support the ministry, especially assisting members who need social support, such as immigrants who have no means of income and are not entitled to any social maintenance from the Government, people who are jobless or homeless, the poor and even the sick. They all need help from the household of faith. The less privileged are the heartbeats of God. The money is meant to be in the house of God as aid.

Giving is crucial for acceptance in the presence of God. Give and it shall be given unto you. Many people like to give to the people that can acknowledge them, or give them reward; also those that can pay them back. These are not God's principles. If you and I give to those that can appreciate us, what is the essence of being a Kingdom Builder?

God is no respecter of anyone, but our creator; he loved both the Jews and the Gentiles, hence believers are the spiritual children of Abraham.

Let's consider the scripture about Haggai (Genesis 21:9 onwards) but in Verse 13 after she was sent away with the lad (Ishmael): ***And also of the son of the bondwoman will I make a nation, because he is thy seed***.

Verses 17-21:

17 *And God heard the voice of the lad; and the angel of God called to Hagar out of heaven, and said unto her, what aileth thee, Hagar? Fear not; for God hath heard the voice of the lad where he is.*

18 *Arise, lift up the lad, and hold him in thine hand; for I will make him a great nation.*

19 *And God opened her eyes, and she saw a well of water; and she went, and filled the bottle with water, and gave the lad drink.*

20 *And God was with the lad; and he grew, and dwelt in the wilderness, and became an archer.*

21 *And he dwelt in the wilderness of Paran: and his mother took him a wife out of the land of Egypt.*

The meaning of the above verses is that God created man in His own image. We are the spiritual seed of Abraham. This event took place when the lad was trying to misbehave in verse 9, was when Sarah requested Abraham to send Hagar and her son away. However, while on a journey the - wilderness experience - both of them went through pain, hunger, thirst and were frustrated, but did not know what to do any more. God is always full of compassion. He was moved by the cry of the lad, and send forth His word to comfort Hagar, hence her eyes could envisage the well of water that was hidden before God intervened. God answered the cry of the lad because he was Abraham's seed.

That does not give you permission to go against your marital vows. It was costly and unhealthy. Jehovah sees and knows what you and I are going through, but trust and obey; in due season, it will not be long, He will answer suddenly. Until you come to realisation and repent from evil ways, returning to God, He will neither leave you nor forsake you. It is just for you to do His will; live a righteous lifestyle and endeavour to please Him for His certificate of approval.

Furthermore, the account of Prophet Isaiah in relation to the attitude towards giving offering/sowing (Isaiah 58: 6-12):

6   *Is not this the fast that I have chosen?
     To loose the bands of wickedness, to
     undo the heavy burdens, and to let the
     oppressed go free, and that ye brake
     every yoke?*

7   *Is it not to deal thy bread to the hungry,
     and that thou bring the poor that are
     cast out to thy house? When thou bring
     seest the naked, that thou cover him;
     and that thou hide not thyself from
     thine own flesh?*

8   *Then shall thy light break forth as the
     morning, and thine health shall spring
     forth speedily: and thy righteousness
     shall go before thee; the glory of the
     LORD shall be thy rearward.*

9   *Then shalt thou call, and the LORD
     shall answer; thou shalt cry and he
     shall say, Here I am. If thou take away
     from the midst of thee the yoke, the
     putting forth of the finger, and speaking
     vanity;*

10   *And if thou draw out thy soul to the
     hungry, and satisfy the afflicted soul;*

then shall thy light rise in obscurity,
and thy darkness be as the noonday:

11 *And the LORD shall guide thee*
continually, and satisfy thy soul in
drought, and make fat thy bones: and
thou shalt be like a watered garden,
and like a spring of water, whose waters
fail not.

12 *And they that shall be of thee shall*
build the old waste places: thou shalt
raise up the foundations of many
generations; and thou shalt be called,
The repairer of the breach, The restorer
of paths to dwell in.

The Lord has given a mandate on giving to the poor, the people in need. Do not simply abstain from food and not being charitable. Drawing people to yourself in giving aid is much more rewarding than selfish gain. When you and I are able to do all the above as analysed with instruction for us to remember the poor, then we shall be authenticated with acceptance. God Himself will rise on your behalf to fight your battle and release help from heaven.

As God did not shut down His eyes on us, we

should do likewise within the families, communities and churches on the local and national level; just be kind and don't shut your mind in doing good. The Lord placed you in that position not for your personal gain but for you to be His ambassador. Let's awaken to the call of God and deviate from anything that is unacceptable towards the kingdom values. You are accountable, but let's repent and do His will, live a life that is pleasing unto God for acceptance.

Furthermore, as acknowledged from the book of Luke (Luke 6:38):

Give, and it shall be given unto you; good measure, pressed down, and shaken together, and running over, shall men given into your bosom. For with the same measure that ye mete withal it shall be measured to you again.

Nevertheless, from the Act of Apostles (Acts 20:35):

I have showed you all things, how that so labouring ye ought to support the weak, and to remember the words of the Lord Jesus, how he said, It is more blessed to give than to receive.

On this notion, this is a specific quotation from

Jesus Christ that is not included within the Gospels. From the Biblical concept, it is vividly true that whenever you give, you are giving because it is a command and mandatory to give. As you release your substance and sow genuinely from your heart, God shall always give seed to the sower and He is a rewarder to replenish the source (Luke 6:38):

This is sensitivity to human relationship with others.

Furthermore, the account of the rich young ruler (Matthew 19:21):

Jesus said unto him, if thou will be perfect, go and sell that thou hast, and give to the poor, and thou shalt have treasure in heaven: and come and follow me.

The rich young ruler was trying to protest that he had kept to the outward demands, but his luxurious wealth and self-righteousness had blinded him to his real weakness. He would not be able to hearken to Jesus for selling his possessions and giving to the poor. He could not afford to sell what he had, but went away sad. This was an indication that he had not kept the commandment, as he loved himself more than he loved his neighbour (the poor) and he loved his possessions more than he loved God thus: not indicating the true discipleship of Christ, but carnality and selfish lifestyle. Let's ponder the account of the Samaritan (Luke 10:30-37):

30 And Jesus answering said, A certain man went down from Jerusalem to Jericho, and fell among thieves, which stripped him of his raiment, and wounded him, and departed, leaving him half dead.

31 And by chance there came down a certain priest that way: and when he saw him, he passed by on the other side.

32 And likewise a Levite, when he was at the place, came and looked on him, and passed by on the other side.

33 But a certain Samaritan, as he journeyed, came where he was: and when he saw him, he had compassion on him,

34 And went to him, and bound up his wounds, pouring in oil and wine, and set him on his own beast, and brought him to an inn, and took care of him.

35 And on the morrow when he departed, he took out two pence, and gave them to the host, and said unto him, Take care of him; and whatsoever thou spendest more, when I come again, I will repay thee.

36 Which now of these three, thinkest thou, was neighbour unto him that fell among the thieves?

37 And he said, He that showed mercy on him. Then said Jesus unto him, Go, and do thou likewise.

Jesus was trying to demonstrate that it was not only ritual attentions which may have been established by the priest and Levite that were the excuses for not stopping to check what was happening. It might be the avoidance of armed robbers on the path where the man was attacked. Nevertheless, Jesus is telling us that no matter the circumstances, their character and behaviour was inhuman and there was no passion towards their fellow human being. Jesus was demanding His creature to love God, and to do the same to other fellow beings, as He Himself is full of love without any bias. Therefore, the key towards salvation for humanity is that God in His infinite mercy gave us His only Son (John 3:16):

For God so loved the world, that he gave his only begotten Son, that whosoever believeth in him should not perish, but have everlasting life.

There is no doubt that love is both a quality of God that portrayed His existence. Jesus alone is the personification of divine love and the basis of all factual affection. His love is absolute and reliable and does seeks the highest good of others, as demonstrated by the Sacrificial Offering on Calvary for our sins. Hence God first loved us, and similarly we ought to love our fellow human beings. You give in various dimensions such as prayers, time, substances and good communication, all embedded in the love of Christ with no hypocrisy. Thus, in doing His will, by living a life that is pleasing unto God to obtain His approval.

Chapter Five

BENEFITS IN PLEASING GOD

BLESSING / PROSPERITY

———=◇◇◇=———

There are benefits towards pleasing God as people who impacted their world have been supernaturally blessed, for example Joseph, Abraham, Noah, Job, Esther, Rahab and the Apostle Paul. These people are among a few in both the Old and New Testaments. They were faithful, obedient to God's commandment, refused to compromise and were able to forgive, giving resources and time and interceding in prayers all in honour unto God. I will deliberate on Joseph, who was among those people blessed by God (Genesis 39:2-4):

2   *And the Lord was with Joseph, and he was a prosperous man; and he was in the house of his master the Egyptian.*

3   *And his master saw that the LORD was with him, and that the LORD made all that he did to prosper in his hand*

4   *And Joseph found grace in his sight, and he served him: and he made him overseer over his house, and all that he had he put into his hand*

The most important aspect was that Joseph's whole life was expressed in the words that the Lord was with him and God made him prosper. He went through trials and temptations that any believer might be going through, but he refused to compromise, as stated in Genesis 39:7:

And it came to pass after these things, that his master's wife cast her eyes upon Joseph; and she said, Lie with me.

Joseph was promoted next to the King and he

was in charge of everything except Potiphar's wife. Many out there in same manner of authority have fallen, but he declined the offer from his master's wife. Though given everything to be in charge, the offer was only one aspect that was forbidden to him. That was where he was being tested, but he was aware that this evil intention was an act of wickedness, regarded as a sin against God.

This type of incident has happened to many people in authority like Joseph, but others have betrayed their masters. The truth of the matter was that because he feared God, he was faithful, loving and caring and had a heart of forgiveness towards his brethren when he was sold into slavery. At last, God made him prosper and the dream that originated the problems in his life came to pass; his brethren bowed and honoured God in his life.

Whatever challenges you might be going through, be assured that everything works together for good. Joseph forgave, passed the test and was approved. According to John 8:29:

And he that sent me is with me: the Father hath not left me alone; for I do always those things that please him.

Saints, as you obey His commandment there is certainly the assurance that God will guide all your doing.

Prayers/interceding

Secondly, as you live a pleasing life, doing His will as commanded, when you call upon Him surely God will answer your prayers. No matter what, try as much as possible to repent from ungodly lifestyles as mentioned earlier in this book. Without holiness no man can please God, and this awakening message is addressed to individuals, families, congregations, communities and nations. Consider your ways and change from your old lifestyle as indicated towards the Seven Churches, so when we pray, intercede for God to answer. The Lord clearly stated in the following verses (John 15: 7,14-17):

7   *If ye abide in me, and my words abide in you, ye shall ask what ye will, and it shall be done unto you.*

14 *Ye are my friend, if ye do whatsoever I command you.*

15 Henceforth I call you not servants; for the servant knoweth not what his lord doeth: but I have called you friends; for all things that I have heard of my Father I have made known unto you.

16 Ye have not chosen me, but I have chosen you, and ordained you, that ye should go and bring forth fruit, and that your fruit should remain: that whatsoever ye shall ask of the Father in my name, he may give it you.

17 These things I command you, that ye love one another.

The description of a vine specifies the nature of our relationship with Jesus, and was a demonstration of fruitful lifestyles in love as the epitome of Christ disciples.

Inheritance

Thirdly, pleasing God will grant you the assurance of getting to your promised land of inheritance (Isaiah 54:3):

For thou shalt break forth on the right hand and on the left; and thy seed shall inherit the Gentiles, and make the desolate cities to be inhabited.

This implies to believers that whatever humiliation you must have gone through shall be forgotten and God will intervene with deep compassion and recall His people with intimacy. Hence, saints shall rejoice in the coming glory as we obey His commandment as mentioned earlier. Also (Isaiah 14:2):

And the people shall take them, and bring them to their place: and the house of Israel shall possess them in the land of the LORD for servants and handmaids: and they shall take them captives, whose captives they were; and they shall rule over their oppressors.

This is a song of triumph. In due season, believers, the spiritual Israel shall be restored in their own land. Therefore, people of God, strive to obey His commandment, do His will, as illustrated earlier, and let your lifestyles reflect Christ for the propagation of the gospel towards a glorious ending.

This book will further discuss the raised concerns in regard to the characteristics classified in the vision towards some named churches which will be inculcated in the message of John to the

Seven Churches. However, this is for our warning and awakening at this present era for us to bring our families, communities, churches and nations back to God. To be accepted is for believers' endeavour to live a life that is pleasing unto God in order to obtain an approval.

Chapter Six

MESSAGE TO THE ANGEL OF THE SEVEN CHURCHES
(REVELATION CHAPTERS 2-3)

———◆———

This was a vision from God to Apostle John to document what was revealed to him about the Seven Churches, namely Ephesus, Smyrna, Pergamum, Thyatira, Sardis, Philadelphia and Laodicea. Some were located in a country identified as Turkey, and others in Asia Minor. They were selected due to issues that contradict things of God.

In regard to these particular two chapters it was laid on the historical explanations towards John's writing. Its emphasis was very descriptive towards the essential raised concerns within the gathering of the children of God, even at this period. Therefore, this is a "wake-up call". They were distinct as a result of the characteristics clarified in the message of John. From these churches we perceived the picture of modern flocks, with various developments within the New Covenant age. The most important thing is for the Saints of God to understand that these two chapters (Revelation 2 and 3) are primarily the revelation of Jesus Christ Himself raising awareness among believers to consider their way of life and for them to change. This could be a warning either directly to an individual or cooperate gathering and summarily with the repeated phrase thus (Revelation 2: 11):

He that hath an ear, let him hear what the Spirit saith unto the churches; He that overcometh shall not be hurt of the second death.

The concept is about doing the will of God and living a lifestyle that is pleasing God for an acceptance, because without holiness no man can please God. The awakening is for saints to consider ways and to live righteously as it was from the beginning; during the time of Noah he pleased God and was approved. The awareness is for us to reflect on our standard ways of living for amendment if not in tune with God commandment. The question is, are you lukewarm, or backsliding, or living an unpleasant lifestyle? May I suggest that you please examine yourself, and endeavour to make every effort to do His will in order to attain His approval.

Let's ponder on the letter addressed to the Churches as follows. The first letter was addressed to the church at Ephesus, (Rev: 2: 1-7):

1 *Unto the angel of the church of Ephesus write: These things saith he that holdeth the seven stars in his right hand, who walketh in the midst of the seven golden candlesticks.*

2 *I know thy works, and they labour, and thy patience, and how thou canst not bear them which are evil: and thou hast tried them which say they are apostles, and are not, and has found them liars.*

3   And hast borne, and hast patience, and for my name's sake hast labored, and hast not fainted.

4   Nevertheless I have somewhat against thee, because thou has left thy first love.

5   Remember therefore from whence thou are fallen, and repent, and do the first works; or else I will come unto thee quickly, and will remove thy candlestick out of this place, except thou repent.

6   But this thou hast, that thou hatest the deeds of the Nicolaitans, which I also hate.

7   He that hath an ear, let him hear what the Spirit saith unto the churches; To him that overcometh will I give to eat of the tree of life, which is in the midst of the paradise of God.

It implies that these groups of churches are hard workers. They persevered, rejected wicked devices, endured pain but had left their first love. The same conduct is found among brethren of this period. The Lord is addressing believers and to be approved of Him, you need to dwell in love;

without the love of Christ, no one can please God. You need to demonstrate the love of Christ. If you don't love, you are not of God's Kingdom, because you cannot give what you don't have. Hence, the demonstration of the love of God is love for people thus, God's people in the assemblies of God (1st John 4:20). Jesus was sinless, surrendered Himself and sacrificed His blood due to love for humanity. This was clearly stated in (John 3:16):

For God so loved the world and gave His only begotten Son, that whosoever believeth in him should not perish but have everlasting life.

"Jesus Himself is Love." God in His mercy gave His only Son for humanity. What have you got to give? The gift of God in you that you can utilize to impact the world. We can emulate Christ in various aspects such as that smile, or a phone call, not for mockery nor for gossiping, but it can mean a lot to somebody's life and any little support goes a long way. Further, to show kindness, in hospitality, caring, sharing etc. you are able to share with one another. You are able to lift other brethren's burden, to be a helper of destiny, not a destroyer, and to be your brother/sister's keeper, and as you do all this not for self-gain but for the love of Christ. All will be on your good record. Hence, believer must not fall into the same unrighteous life that makes God grieve towards His people. The message is a wake-up call for us, as stated: (Rev: 2:7a)

He that hath an ear, let him hear what the Spirit saith unto the churches.

The Spirit of God was addressing the named churches of concern, as revealed by Apostle John, so also addressing all churches in every race and age till the coming of Christ.

We need to adhere to the voice of God, as it was a promise of mercy to those who overcame. Christian life is a battle against sin, Satan, the world and the flesh. For example an episode between Balak (the king) and Balaam (the prophet) was secular and spiritual because Balaam would have cursed Israel as requested by Balak, if not by divine intervention of God, as Balaam was a man who loved money (Numbers 22:5-Chapter23). Nonetheless, it shows how some believers do compromise because of materialism. The Lord is raising awareness against negative characteristics within the house of God. Bribery, corruption, injustice etc reign all over the world. It is not enough that we engage in warfare; we must never yield to our spiritual enemies, as Balak was pressurizing Balaam to curse the people of God. We have to fight the good fight of faith till we gain victory, and that is what persevering Christians should do.

Not until the Lord intervened and opened the eyes of Balaam did he realized God was in control and monitoring the affairs between him and the king for him to curse the people whom the Lord had blessed (Numbers 23:7- 8). Nonetheless, Balaam refused to yield to Balak's request because he was the king. Therefore, Christian warfare shall have a glorious and triumphant reward. This was the promise to the victors: that they shall eat of the tree of life which is in the midst of the paradise of God (Revelation 2:7). They shall have that perfection of holiness that Adam would have had if he had obeyed the commandment of God. So we should persevere in this journey of faith and endeavour to live a pleasing life to inherit the Kingdom of Heaven and reign with Christ.

The message to the Smyrna was that they were the persecuted church (Revelation 2:8-11). The church went through suffering, poverty and persecution, which is an ongoing situation in this present age. You were not permitted to share Christ publicly such as in the workplace, schools, shopping centres, etc., but the Lord desired us to remain faithful because He is always with us. He acknowledged our needs. He Himself has experienced suffering as we have. Whatever you are going through, Jesus has been there too. He is alive at all times with us and there shall be no more sorrow (Revelation 21:4). He is reassuring and encouraging all believers that they should keep the fire burning, Jesus is glorified. From (Rev 2:8-11)

8. *And unto the angel of the church in Smyrna write; These things saith the first and the last, which was dead, and is alive;*

9. *I know thy works, and tribulations and poverty, (but thou art rich) and I know the blasphemy of them which say they are Jews, and are not, but are the synagogue of Satan.*

10. *Fear none of those things which thou shalt suffer: behold the devil shall cast some of you into prison, that ye may be*

*tried; and yea shall have tribulations
ten days; be thou faithful unto death,
and I will give thee a crown of life.*

*11. He that hath an ear, let him hear what
the Spirit saith unto the churches. He
that overcometh shall not be hurt of the
second death.*

Jesus is telling believers that there will be persecution, but not to be discouraged even unto death, as He was persecuted even by some of the elect. Although the persecution will be a product of Christ's precious gift to those that abide to His commandment, they will be crowned in glory. However, Jesus reproves their failures, and rewards their faithfulness. Therefore, this is a universal "wake up call" so that all His creation should hear what Christ is saying to his churches, that He will save all his faithful servants. As a result, the first death shall not hurt them, and the second death shall have no power over the overcomers.

Christ implored believers to persevere. No matter what challenges you face, you must not give up. You must keep pressing on, because at the end you shall be commended with a reward.

This is an awakening for us to abide in His commandment, and a gracious promise to overcomers. He that overcomes shall not be hurt by the second death (Revelation 2:11).

To the Pergamum church (Rev. 2:12-17):

12 *And to the angel of the church in Pergamos write: These things saith he which hath that sharp sword with two edges;*

13 *I know thy works, and where thou dwellest, even where Satan's seat is: and thou holdest fast my name, and hast not denied my faith even in those days wherein Antipas was my faithful martyr, who was slain among you, where Satan dwelleth.*

14. *But I have a few things against thee, because thou has there them that hold the doctrine of Balaam, who taught Balak to cast a stumbling block before the children of Israel, to eat, things sacrificed unto idols, and to commit fornication.*

15. *So hast thou also them that hold the doctrine of the Nicolaitans, which thing I hate.*

16. Repent; or else I will come unto thee quickly, and will fight against them with the sword of my mouth.

17. He that hath an ear, let him hear what the Spirit saith unto the churches; To him that overcometh will I give to eat of the hidden manna, and will give him a white stone, and in the stone a new name written, which no man knoweth saving he that receiveth it.

These churches are morally compromised. They keep on truthful, faithful to death, but they still tolerate sins such as immorality, adultery, fornication, lust, blasphemy and unholy living. They settle for worldly activities (materialism), and word came for them to repent (verse 16), otherwise He will come unto them to fight them with the sword. Consequently, the same message is applicable to believers to change for virtuous lifestyles and deviate from covetousness. We should not settle for less because of selfish interests and endeavour to speak the truth; though it is not pleasant, it prevails. The Lord is passing this message to all ages and races, to try as much as possible to be disciplined and change from all unrighteousness, and live a holy life in love as Jesus loved humanity.

I want to suggest to the pastors/leaders, even myself, for everyone to speak the Word of Truth; if at all the tithe and offering bag are affected, you still need to preach the gospel truth and there should not be any compromise, because you are accountable to God who has called you, and be aware that without holiness no one can please the Lord.

Furthermore, the Thyatira church was the doctrinally and compromising group (Rev: 2: 18-29):

18. *And unto the angel of the church in Thyatira write: These things saith the Son of God, who hath his eyes like unto a flame of fire, and his feet are like fine brass;*

19. *I know thy works, and charity, and service, and faith, and thy patience, and thy works; and the last to be more than the first.*

20. *Notwithstanding I have a few things against thee, because thou sufferest that woman Jezebel, which calleth herself a prophetess, to teach and to seduce my*

servants to commit fornication, and to eat things sacrificed unto idols.

21. And I gave her space to repent of her fornication, and she repented not.

22. Behold, I will cast her into a bed, and them that commit adultery with her into great tribulation, except they repent of their deeds.

23. And I will kill her children with death; and all the churches shall know that I am he which searcheth the reins and hearts: and I will give unto every one of you according to your works.

24. But unto you I say, and unto the rest in Thyatira, as many as have not this doctrine, and which have not known the depths of Satan, as they speak; I will put upon you none other burden.

25. But that which ye have already hold fast till I come.

26. And he that overcometh, and keepeth my works unto the end, to him will I give power over the nations:

27. AND HE SHALL RULE THEM WITH A ROD OF IRON; AS THE VESSELS OF A POTTER SHALL THEY BE BROKEN TO SHIVERS: even as I received of my Father.

28. And I will give him the morning star.

29. He that hath an ear, let him hear what the Spirit saith unto the churches.

The doctrinally compromising church has all sorts of unrighteous living like corruption, fornication, idolatry, dishonesty, and materialism. Hence, no sinner can behold His glory, even as they teach false doctrine. The Lord raised a warning to His people through John for the leaders (angels) of the church to hold unto the truth because there are consequences for not abiding to His commandment. As inscribed in the Law of Moses that is embedded in the New commandment (John 13:34):

A new commandment I give unto you, That ye love one another as I have loved you, that ye also love one another.

Therefore, let him hear what the Spirit saith unto the churches.

Saints, if you don't love you will be tempted

and fall into committing adultery. You can steal, kill and destroy, which was declared by John 10:10:

The thief cometh not, but for to steal, and to kill, and to destroy: I am come that they might have life, and that they might have it more abundantly.

So the thief mentioned above signifies the devil, which could be represented in various features. Hence Rev: 2: 26-29 implies the promise with generosity and recompense that will be given to the persevering and triumphant church, thus the overcomers.

Nonetheless, let us ponder Verse 20-23 on the account of Baxter from the vision given to her by God towards "Revelation in Hell". That shall not be our portion, in Jesus' Mighty Name Amen. As heaven is real, so also is hell. This is a wake-up call and cautioning. The verses signify seducing spirits within the gathering of saints. It is of concern that this is happening within some Christian gatherings at this era. How can we win souls for the Kingdom of God, when your attitude towards your brother/sister is not portraying Christ? You are the Bible that unbelievers are reading. You confide in your brethren, and before you realized it the news is all over the gathering. That little object (your tongue) is crucial to make or break your brethren. Saints, awake and let us be our brothers'/sisters' keeper. Jesus has paid the price on the Cross of Calvary. We do not need to nail Him back on the cross again. Love your neighbor as yourself even as Jesus loves you. The upright shall have dominion as Jesus declared (verse 28): *"I will give him the morning star".* Christ is the morning star, that crown of glory.

Nonetheless, Sardis were the fake church (Rev. 3:1-6):

1. *And unto the angel of the church in Sardis write; These things saith he that hath the seven Spirits of God, and the seen stars; I know thy works, that thou has a name that thou livest, and art dead.*

2. *Be watchful, and strengthen the things which remain, that are ready to die: for I have not found thy works perfect before God.*

3. *Remember therefore how thou hast received and heard, and hold fast, and repent, if therefore thou shalt not*

watch. I will come on thee as a thief,
and thou shall not know what hour I
will come upon thee.

4. *Thou hast a few names even in Sardis*
   which have not defiled their garments;
   and they shall walk with me in white for
   they are worthy.

5. *He that overcometh, the same shall be*
   clothed in white raiment; and I will not
   blot out his name out of the book of life;
   but I will confess his name before my
   Father, and before his angels.

6. *He that hath an ear, let him hear what*
   the Spirit saith unto the churches.

The above named church has a reputation as if they were alive, but they are already dead in all their doings (the counterfeit church). Just like this generation, many go to a church but not a Bible-believing church, more or less a social gathering. The word of God declared in Verse 1: "I know thy work..." you act as if you are alive, but you are already dead in deeds. They are not a measure of God's approval; their standards are far from Christianity. Although physically you might think you are doing the will of God, from the spiritual perspective you are not living a life that is pleasing unto Him to obtain approval. Your church might help the less privileged or heal the sick, with a negative mindset for self-gain, but that is not according to His will because He knows your motive behind everything. You might be doing for selfish gain, but it is warning saints to repent, and teach your members the doctrine towards holiness.

If you are looking for men's glory because the glory of God has departed, please try to repent your sins. Do not let the light of God in you diminish if no repentance from self-glory, manipulation, etc. It is time to arise, be at alert, living holy and fear the Lord for tomorrow might be too late (verse 3). Some received Christ and remain faithful in readiness, while some did not, as the account of the Ten (10 virgins) (Matthew 25:1-13):

1   *Then shall the kingdom of heaven be likened unto ten virgins, which took their lamps, and went forth to meet the bridegroom.*

2   *And five of them were wise, and five were foolish.*

3 *They that were foolish took their lamps, and took no oil with them:*

4 *But the wise took oil in their vessels with their lamps.*

5 *While the bridegroom tarried, they all slumbered and slept.*

6 *And at midnight there was a cry made, Behold, the bridegroom cometh; go ye out to meet him.*

7 *Then all those virgins arose, and trimmed their lamps.*

8 *And the foolish said unto the wise, Give us your oil; for our lamps are gone out.*

9 *But the wise answered, saying, Not so; lest there be not enough for us and you: but go ye rather to them that sell, and buy for yourselves.*

10 *And while they went to buy, the bridegroom came; and they that were ready went in with him to the marriage; and the door was shut.*

11 *Afterward came also the other virgins, saying, Lord, Lord open to us.*

**12 But he answered and said, Verily I say
unto you, I know you not.**

**13 Watch therefore, for ye know neither the
day not the hour wherein the Son of
man cometh.**

Various events are signalling the end times as
recorded in the Scriptures, such as wars,
earthquakes, disturbances, famine, pestilence etc.
The awareness is for the believer to be awake and
to be ready, for tomorrow might be too late. The
account as stated above is for us to do his will
while other concerns shall be resolved, as nobody
knows when the bridegroom shall arrive. No one
informed the Virgins of the specific time the
bridegroom would arrive. We should all strive to
be watchful because we never know when the
bridegroom will come according to the stated
Scripture (Matthew 25:13). You must be extra
careful and vigilant. The foolish virgins were
careless while the wise ones were vigilant and
careful. So, they were chosen because they
focused, awaiting their guest. This is an
awakening message by one of the Epistle of
Apostle Paul (Ephesians 6:13-15):

13. Wherefore take unto you the whole armour of God, that ye may be able to withstand in the evil day, and having done all, to stand.

14. Stand therefore, having your loins girt about with truth, and having on the breastplate of righteousness;

15. And your feet shod with the preparation of the gospel of peace.

The idea is, when you have done all things to stand, you still need to be steadfast, patient and sensitive, because you never know what tomorrow will have in store. Saints, you need to be watchful and be thoughtful to things of the spirit (Philippians 3:13-14). As you move from one level to another, the target is "ever upward". Hence, laying your hands on the plough, you cannot look back. As we believed, and made that decision to follow Jesus all the way through, there is no looking back, although there are worldly activities that could cause distractions, so we need to be vigilant and stand for Jesus. The ultimate goal is do His will, live a righteous living, and live a life that is agreeable unto God's standard for His authorization.

From the ten virgins account, five were wise virgins, and they were accepted. They got themselves prepared and ready for their master's use, while the foolish five were rejected. The question is, are you ready for the master's acceptance?

Baxter (1997) after her visit to Hell stated "Time is running out". Her ordeal, with people screaming from the pit of hell, was described in her book titled *A Divine Revelation of Hell,* in which she categorically stated:

"Friend, if you are living in sin, please repent. If you have been born again and have turned your back on God, repent and turn back to Him now. Live good: and stand for truth. Wake up before it is too late, and you can spend forever with the Lord in heaven".

Jesus responded from one of her encounters: "Hell has a body (like a human form) lying on its back in the centre of the earth. Hell is shaped like a human body – very large and with many chambers of torment". Jesus was imploring Baxter to tell the children of God globally (believers/Christians). The book is penned to raise an awareness as a "wake-up call":

"Remember to tell the people of earth that hell is real. Millions of lost souls are here, and more are coming every day. On the Great Judgement Day, death and hell will be cast into the lake of fire; that will be the second death."

There are men/women of God who had visions in regard to hell or heaven which no doubt are real. We shall end well and condemnation shall not be our portion in Jesus' Mighty name Amen. Therefore, we must be prepared, be awake, and examine ourselves, reflects on routine lifestyles, self-awareness and taking precautions not to fall into any temptations. Saints, let's endeavour in seeking God by doing His will, living righteously in preparation for his coming. Our story shall not be of those foolish virgins but rather to emulate Christ, because God loved humanity and gave us His Son; He first loved us (John 3:16). The care of this world is an enemy (the devil) to God. From these events five virgins were ready to do His will, prepared and at alert. They were sensitive to the things of the spirit, seeking God first and all His righteousness and were able to live a well pleasing lifestyle.

Therefore, the emphasis on that phrase "He that hath ear let him hear what the Spirit said unto the churches" is a wake-up call raising a warning against matter of concerns towards the Kingdom of Heaven. As people are living lives that are far from Kingdom principles, except you do His will as demanded, live a life agreeable unto God before an acceptance to obtain His approval. Jesus Christ the same yesterday, and today, and forever (Hebrew 13:8).

Philadelphia is the obedient Church (Rev: 3:7-13):

7. *And to the angel of the church in Philadelphia write; These things saith he that is holy, he that is true, HE THAT HATH THE KEY OF DAVID, HE THAT OPENETH, AND NO MAN SHUTTETH; AND SHUTTETH, AND NO MAN OPENETH;*

8. *I know thy works: behold, I have set before thee an open door, and no man can shut it; for though hast a little strength, and hast kept my word, and hast not denied my name.*

9. *Behold, I will make them of the synagogue of Satan, which say they are Jews, and are not, but do lie; behold, I will make them to come and worship*

before thsy feet, and to know that I have loved thee.

10. *Because thou hast kept the word of my patience, I also will keep thee from the hour of temptation, which shall come upon all the world, to try them that dwell upon the earth.*

11. *Behold, *I come quickly: hold that fast, which thou hast, that no man take thy crown.*

12. *Him that overcometh will I make a pillar in the temple of my God, and he shall go no more out and I will write upon him the name of my God, and the name of the city of my God, which is new Jerusalem, which cometh down out of heaven from my God: and I will write upon him my new name.*

13. *He that hath an ear, let him hear what the Spirit saith unto the churches.*

They possessed little strength, but kept the word of God and walked upright. They endured and patiently honoured God, they lived a life that was pleasing unto God: They were the true church and the professing church, though they experienced persecution, but they still kept the word of God. The Lord is reassuring them that no man will take their crown from them. The Lord is making demands of believers/saints that no matter what you are going through, He sees, and knows your capability. Your strength and weakness He knows. He perceived you from inside and out, just for us to trust and obey his commandment that will enable the endorsement of His signature of authenticity.

Abraham was tested and came out triumphantly, and the same with Job. What about you for his approval with declaration of "welcome faithful servant of God come into my rest"? These were the promises by Our Saviour; a glorious reward is awaiting victorious believers. However, the Spirit of God repeatedly makes a demand of warning: *"He that have an ear, let him hear what the Spirit saith unto the churches"*. How Christ loves and value his faithful people, how He commends, and how they shall be crowned in glory.

The Laodicea church (Rev: 3: 14-22):

14. And unto the angel of the church of the Laodiceans write; These things saith the

Amen, the faithful and true witness, the beginning of the creation of God.

15. I know thy works, that thou art neither cold nor hot: I would thou wert cold or hot.

16. So then because thou art lukewarm, and neither cold nor hot, I will spew thee out of my mouth.

17. Because thou sayest, I am rich; and increased with goods, and have need of nothing; and knowest not that thou art wretched and miserable, and poor, and blind and naked;

18. I counsel thee to buy of me gold tried in the fire, that thou mayest be rich; and white raiment, that thou mayest be clothed, and that the shame of thy nakedness do not appear; and anoint thine eyes with eyesalve, that thou mayest see.

19. As many as I love, I rebuke and chasten: be zealous therefore, and repent.

20. Behold, I stand at the door, and knock: if any man hear my voice, and open the door; I will come in to him, and will sup with him, and he with me.

21. To him that overcometh will I grant to sit with me in my throne, even as I also overcome, and am set down with my Father in his throne,

22. He that hath an ear, let him hear what the Spirit saith unto the churches.

This was the materialist group, like some churches of this generation. The Lord is speaking because we are the church. It does not matter who you are, for God is no respecter of any person. They were neither cold nor hot, the lukewarm groups, they have been deceived by Satan. We pray that God should revive His people (Galatians 5:19-21). Carnal-mindedness, like adultery, fornication, uncleanness, lasciviousness, witchcraft, hatred, with seducing flesh, even heresies can never please God. Although the people of Laodicea were wealthy physically or materially, spiritually they were poor. Therefore the awakening is for all believers to change and repent from all evil practices, though this is applicable to all generations.

Hebrew 13:8: ***Jesus is the same yesterday, and today, and forever.***

Brethren, even in the midst of any circumstances, live holy, hold your faith, don't copy ideology or philosophy. Be mindful, focus and be heavenly bound. On the day of reckoning it is not a matter of Pastor or members; each shall give account at the throne of God. Rise and be on fire for God continually.

This is the messages of Christ to the churches, which is applicable to churches of all ages. Some people come with lukewarm self-confidence, yet it is possible that by the reproofs and counsels of Christ they might be inspired with renewed mind, and enabled to overcome any warfare. By being born again, given their lives to Christ, if they did so all former faults should be forgiven, and they would have a great reward. This awakening is to all churches of Christ in every race and ages all over the universe. This is happening in all subsequent churches, so they may acknowledge how God will deal with any church as He dealt with those seven designated churches which are examples and applicable to all global churches even at this period. God sent His message via

Apostle John to those churches as an example, warning the entire congregation to put into considerations what they may envisage to receive from God, and what those who are disloyal may expect to undergo from the Lord on the day of accountability. Therefore noticeably, the repeated phrase (Revelation 3:22): *He that hath an ear, let him hear what the Spirit saith unto the churches.*

I suggest, Saints, to change from unholy living so that a certificate of approval can be obtained. As the Lord has raised this awareness remember: that He is still the same and He never changed (Hebrew 13:8).

Chapter Seven

PASTORS/LEADERS

———◇———

Christianity is real, and the church of God will stand for ever. This is a wake-up call for humanity. As it was in the beginning from Genesis to the end of the book of Revelations is also for our consciousness. As the way of life revealed by Apostle John to the angels of the seven churches, the same is applicable to the angels of this generation.

Angels stand for the leaders within authority, such as apostles, prophets, evangelists, pastors, and teachers. The message is in two dimensions, both the spiritual and the secular authority; all positions are governed by God. Hence, ministers are to preach the word of God, to act, live by it, and act as a role model. Saints of God, we cannot separate the Old from the New Testament. because it is all written with the inspiration of the Holy Spirit. Without holiness, no man can please God. The Lord is telling us to prepare to meet Him and He is coming soon. The question is, are you ready? Therefore, let's make every effort to live a life pleasing unto God for His approval.

To obtain His approval means giving up the self and becoming perfect before God. Jesus gave up Himself with His sacrificial offering for our salvation. He gave up His life and experienced what the saints have encountered or challenges that human beings might be going through. Jesus Christ "humbled himself, and became obedient unto death". Therefore, this is an awareness for us to be "awake" at this end time to preach the undiluted word of truth to the congregation as instructed by the power of the Holy Spirit. Hence, I want to suggest we live a holy lifestyle to emulate Christ in order to portray righteous living, and heavenly conscience in obedience, doing His will. Therefore, the following criteria need to be in place.

The Wisdom of God

This message is addressing leaders, both in spiritual and secular authority. To ministers of the gospel, I will suggest that we should try to preach the undiluted Word of God, "Truth" to please God but not unto men, and we need to pray and also seek for this divine wisdom that is the vital tool (Proverbs 4:7):

Wisdom is the principal thing; therefore get wisdom: and with all thy getting get understanding.

I will recommend that we all strive to live a life that give pleasure to God, which is a choice by an individual but a requirement by Him. Let's see (Malachi 3: 16-18):

16 Then they that feared the LORD spake often one to another: and the LORD hearkened, and heard it, and a book of remembrance was written before him for them that feared the LORD, and that thought upon his name.

17 And they shall be mine, saith the LORD of hosts, in that day when I make up my jewels; and I will spare them, as a man spareth his own son that serveth him.

18 Then shall ye return, and discern between the righteous and the wicked, between him that serveth God and him that serveth him not.

Thus the application of wisdom and the fear of the Lord in order to have an intimacy with God and man is the way forward in doing His will, because we are accountable. Let's have a closer look on the account of King Solomon in his wisdom; he was able to judge rightly when the two harlots brought their case (1st King 3: 16-21, and 24-26):

16 Then came there two women, that were harlots, unto the king, and stood before him.

17 And the one woman said, O my lord, I and this woman dwell in one house; and I was delivered of a child with her in the house,

18 And it came to pass the third day after that I was delivered, that this woman was delivered also; and we were together; there was no stranger with us in the house, save we two in the house.

19 And this woman's child died in the night; because she overlaid it.

*20 And she arose at midnight, and took my
son from beside me. While thine
handmaid slept, and laid it in her
bosom, and laid her dead child in my
bosom.*

*21 And when I rose in the morning to give
my child suck, behold, it was dead: but
when I had considered it in the
morning, behold, it was not my son,
which I did bear.*

At this contemporary era, many souls have been wasted due to injustice. Wisdom and justice were highly esteemed qualities of a good leader, when you are able to distinguish between good and bad, as the character and the attitude of the woman that exchanged the dead child for the living one was identified as wickedness. Therefore leaders, before discharging any decision, do your utmost to search for the truth before passing any judgement. So many disorderly lifestyles are happening in households of faith, within societies, families, even nations, at the market places. Therefore, either at home, in the workplace, or the house of God truth is a vital utensil. King Solomon applied wisdom to deal with this sensitive dispute.

I will suggest that we all should pray for the manifold wisdom of God that rule the earth.

Furthermore, from verses 24-26:

24 *And the king said, Bring me a sword. And they brought a sword before the king.*

25 *And the king said, Divide the living child in two, and give half to the one, and half to the other.*

26 *Then spake the woman whose the living child was unto the king, for her bowels yearned upon her son, and she said, O my lord, give her the living child, and in no wise slay it. But the other said, Let it be neither mine nor thine, but divide it.*

In various situations, wicked people do not care. It was due to carelessness that this woman laid over her child, and she got no heart by demanding the child to be sliced in two, because she had nothing to lose. The second woman knew that in due season, the truth would be revealed and prevail over the dilemma; while the King decided not to slice the living child. On the other hand, with the manifold wisdom applied by the king, he was able to resolve the critical and sensitive incident amicably. The king must have psychologically observed that this woman was telling lies, either by her appearance, body language, and aggressiveness, even her tone while narrating the incident with her nonchalant and callous attitude. The King was able to apply the wisdom of God to perceive the evil act.

People of God, men/women in authority should endeavor to attain wisdom, this is the principal thing. Evil is reigning all over the earth; we pray for the Mercy of God to reign supreme. According to Ecclesiastes 12:14:

For God shall bring every work into judgment, with every secret thing, whether it be good, or whether it be evil.

As a leader, even it is applicable to everyone, be assured that the controlling factor of life should be in the fear of God, doing His will, and living a well-pleasing lifestyle that will authenticate approval, which is the ultimate goal.

Furthermore, according to Ecclesiastes 9:11 & 15:

I returned, and saw under the sun, that the race is not to the swift, nor the battle to the strong, neither yet bread to the wise, nor yet riches to men of understanding, nor yet favour to men of skill; but time and chance happeneth to them all.

15 *Now there was found in it a poor wise man, and he by his wisdom delivered the city, yet no man remembered that same poor man.*

Man/woman in position of authority please, I will propose that you let truth prevail, please utilize the authority given to you to act as an ambassador of Christ. Also, to kindly engage in truth in your routine activities and suggest not to execute agenda that could have a negative impact on the poor, the less privileged, as you abide to the commandment of God, because in most instances the voices of the poor masses are not being heard.

Empathy

Jesus Christ was born in a manger (Luke 2:15-16):

15 *And it came to pass, as the angels were gone away from them into heaven, the shepherds said one to another, Let us now go even unto Bethlehem, and see this thing which is come to pass which the Lord hath made known unto us.*

16 And they came with haste and found
Mary, and Joseph, and the babe lying in
a manger.

He is a typical example for humanity. He was the Master, but acted as the servant, so that we could imitate Him. Jesus became poor so that we might be rich. This group are the heartbeat of God, please I advocate that you govern and lead people accordingly in the fear of the Lord. Do not compromise; many injustices have been executed without proper findings. The Lord is warning His people to treat people the way they want them to be treated. Please have compassion and avoid hypocrisy, as the characteristics signified within the seven churches are for our warning for us not to be a victim.

The question is: What legacy will you leave behind? For example, the parable of the Good Samaritan; does it apply to you? Do you really care about people around you? Additionally, words are powerful. Some lives have been truncated due to negative words to a fellow being. The smallest object of the system is your tongue. How did you utilize it with people? Is it to enhance, empower, encourage, pray for people or to do otherwise? As leader, pastor, departmental head, manager etc within the secular and spiritual realm, while people confide in you as their advocator, but before due season, the concealed information has circulated all over. No wonder! Many Christians are suffering in silence. There are very few disciplined and trustworthy people within the body of Christ, even secular groups to lean on. Nevertheless there are still some righteous servants of God, good mentors, advocators, counsellors and managers that could be referred to as the (angels) across the Globe, those that are ready to support in one capacity or the other either via mentoring, giving, counselling, advocator, prayer etc., Nonetheless, let love reign, for Jesus is Love.

People of God, due to lack of love, nations have been demoralized globally, hatred between brother and sister, betrayal of trust, unable to forgive, jealousy, gossiping, idolatry, fornicators, wickedness of all sorts. Then, how would evangelism to win the unbelievers be effective? What are you fighting or struggling for? The world is created by God Himself. According to 1st Corinthians 2: 9:

But as it is WRITTEN, EYE HATH NOT SEEN, NOR EAR HEARD, NEITHER HAVE ENTERED INTO THE HEART OF MAN, THE THINGS WHICH GOD HATH PREPARED FOR THEM THAT LOVE HIM.

We should not forget that all the human race originated from one parent (Abraham). He is the father of both the Jews and the Arabs (Genesis 12:1), but God set confusion to the human race at the event when people created by Him were trying to build a tower known as the Tower of Babel to compete with their Creator. Hence, God in His sovereign power set misunderstanding and scattered the plan of mankind in their craftiness. Therefore, diverse tongues and language surfaced (Genesis 11:7-9):

7   *God to, let us go down, and there confound their language, that they may not understand one another's speech.*

8   *So the LORD scattered them abroad from thence upon the face of all the earth: and they left off to build the city.*

9   *Therefore is the name of it called Babel; because the LORD did there confound the language of all the earth: and from thence did the LORD scatter them abroad upon the face of all the earth.*

People of God, let love prevail in all our deeds and fear Him continually. When there is unity, prayers are answered speedily, then God will be happy with His people. However, there is always confusion in godless society or within the congregation of His children, so, God is warning against these ill act. We should note that whatever you do to the least of your brother, you are simply doing it unto God. Saints of God should strive to let love be supremacy, and treat fellowmen like yourself. Whoever you are, we are God's creation: let brotherly love continue.

Awareness

A wake-up call entails adhering to total commandment in obedience to God, doing His will, and to love one another. Please let us try to treat others as you would like to be treated, avoid compromise and deviate from the bribery and corruption that are ruling the world. Endeavour not to be a man-pleaser as King Saul lost his throne due to people's pressure and he displeased God (1st Samuel 15:24-31). Conversely, the repeated word of God to his people as stated in Revelation 2:11:

He that hath an ear, let him hear what the Spirit saith unto the churches: He that overcometh shall not be hurt of the second death.

The word of God is encouraging His saints to be faithful and to persevere through pressure and trials of life. Thereafter they will gain an approval, while the unbelievers will be destroyed from the second death. Jesus Christ is still the same, He changed not. As it was warning during the time of Noah (1st Peter 3: 19-20):

19 By which also he went and preached unto the spirits in prison;

19 Which sometime were disobedient, when once the longsuffering of God waited in the days of Noah, while the ark was a preparing wherein few, that is, eight souls were saved by water.

I beseech you people of God, to try your best to obey His commandment, in order to make Him happy rather to please men.

Forgiveness

People of God, try as much as possible to forgive,

not holding anyone in captivity within your heart, nor keeping malice. You had better let go and forgive, and forget about the old pathway. Meditate on the Lord's prayers and you will see the essence of forgiveness (Matthew 6:9-15):

9   *After this manner therefore pray ye: Our Father which art in heaven, Hallowed be thy name.*

10   *Thy kingdom come, Thy will be done in earth, as it is in heaven.*

11   *Give us this day our daily bread*

12   *And forgive us our debts, as we forgive our debtors.*

13   *And lead us not into temptation, but deliver us from evil: For thine is the kingdom and the power, and the glory, forever. Amen.*

14   *For if ye forgive men their trespasses, your heavenly Father will also forgive you.*

15   *But if ye forgive not men their trespasses, neither will your Father forgive your trespasses.*

The heart of forgiveness towards one another was emphasized by Jesus Christ so that prayers cannot be hindered. Many are going through health problems due to issues or concerns being bottled up, thereby affecting the whole system. The Lord is commanding that it is a mandatory principle to forgive so that you can obtain His approval, as heaven is real, the same is hell.

God is raising people to minister universally, an awareness that would enable believers to be ready for His coming. As people are busy with routine activities and living unrighteousness during the period of Noah while he was constructing the Ark, he was warning people to repent from their old pathway. The same is applicable to people at this time. Men and women of God are implored to raise their voices to preach the undiluted word of truth to their congregations, members, communities to change from sinful acts such as backsliding, immorality, adultery, fornication, lust, blasphemy, hatred against one another, unforgiveness, envy, bloodshed, etc. Conversely, to live a pleasing lifestyle is to love one and another not for selfish interests, nor being hypocritical, but love in action, to be passionate, to have compassion. Jesus humbled Himself throughout His earthly ministry till death. Please let us try to be humble, at the same time being assertive. Let your yea be yea and fear God. When fear is embedded in each one of us, you will not plan nor harm your neighbour.

John 3: 16b: *That whosoever believeth in him should not perish, but have eternal life*.

Saints, this awakening is to raise the alertness of the Lord's coming so that believers would not be taken unaware. As He declared in John 16:33b:

In the world ye shall have tribulation: but be of good cheer, I have overcome the world.

Saints, as we strived to live as demanded by God, in His infinite mercy and grace we shall inherit everlasting life. For that reason, Revelation 3: 22 specified:

He that hath an ear, let him hear what the Spirit saith unto the churches.

The above line is the repeated phrase in the message to the Seven Churches and is applicable to the angels of churches and organization of this time.

He never changes: *Jesus Christ the same yesterday, and today, and forever* (Hebrew 13:8).

Be watchful

Christianity should not be like the story of those five foolish virgins (Matthew 25: 1-13). Due to carelessness and unpreparedness they ran out of oil; they were not watchful and instead of keeping the oil burning continually before the arrival of the bridegroom, they were faithless as He had been promising his arrival for a while but never came, so they were not ready. Saints, for our race not to be a similar case, let's be vigilant.

Luke 12:35-40 was demonstrating the word of Jesus, declaring that we should seek first the kingdom of God then all others shall be added. From now, believers need to be watchful, gird their loins and "be alert". Therefore, we must examine ourselves, change, and deviate from unholy lifestyles. You and I shall not be rejected on the day of reckoning in the Name of Jesus Christ Amen.

That is the rationale behind this awakening, so that it will not cut anyone unaware of the coming of our Lord. If you felt uncomfortable to do the self-assessment, it is high time to sort out the unrighteousness and change to live a better life that is pleasing unto God, to do His will as commanded for an approval.

Contrarily, let's ponder on the account of King Nebuchadnezzar (Daniel 4: 27-37). He was sent to the animal kingdom and nobody noticed his absence from the palace (Daniel 4:32):

And they shall drive thee from men, and thy dwelling shall be with the beasts of the field: they shall make thee to eat grass as oxen, and seven times shall pass over thee, until thou know that the most High ruleth in the kingdom of men, and giveth it to whosoever he will.

Until the king came to his senses like the prodigal son he squandered all resources he did not struggle for (Luke 15:11-24). The awakening is advising some people in authority that normally maltreat their subordinates because they got the authority, forgetting it is of God that appointed you there. You are who you are, not by your power nor by might but by the Spirit of God. Hence, any position you found yourself is not by your own making but is orchestrated by heaven, and we should be careful how we relate to people around us. Nebuchadnezzar came to cognizance that of a truth God reigns in the affairs of men he bowed to God of heaven and earth. Furthermore, his son Belshazzar came to the throne and repeated the same unrighteous lifestyles; his cruelty was more than that of his father. Daniel the prophet, who was the interpreter of a concealed dream, was consulted again, but before he finished the analysis of the inscribed handwriting on the wall instantly "the voice of the Lord" descended from heaven and the reigning King was rejected (Daniel 5:30): *In that night was Belshazzar the King of the Chaldeans slain.*

Pride

The wealth acquired from the King's perception was that all he had was of his own might, having forgotten that it was God who released the blessing. Warning: please note that no matter the position you attain, you should be conscious that it is not by your power but the power of the Holy Spirit you are placed on that seat of authority. Routinely it is necessary to consider the type of lifestyle we are living if in line with Kingdom principles, and be filled with hearts of gratitude in praising and worshipping Him and forbidding the spirit of "Pride".

The question is, what is the essence of gaining the whole world and losing your precious soul?

King Belshazzar had forgotten that it is only God that is the controller of our lives and is applicable to some dignitaries in various organizations. For example: oppressor, intimidation, betrayal of trust within the body of Christ even in the secular world. So therefore, as it were, God changed not (Hebrew 13:8), additionally, (Daniel 4: 32): *until thou know that most High ruleth in the kingdom of men and giveth it to whosoever he will.* Jesus is still the same because the scripture cannot be broken. Don't think there is none like you. The king was rejected and condemned; we shall not be doomed by our sinful nature that can lead to condemnation before God in Jesus' name Amen.

Let's ponder this incident: it is not everyone that can obtain the grace of "second chance". Beloved, endeavour to do His will, worship Him in fear and trembling, obey His commandment for acceptance.

This "message of awakening" is for anyone in authority; either within the secular or spiritual sphere, to deviate from unholy ways of life like hypocrisy, deceit, betrayal of trust, evil practice, lies, idolatry, bribery, corruption, unforgiveness, unrighteous living etc. God is raising a warning us to stop and change, because tomorrow might be too late. Your attitude, your character towards your fellow brethren, matters a lot because you are the light of the world so that God can be boastful of you. He did on behalf of Job.

The Fear of God

Did you realized that God was demonstrating to Job's friend that he (Job) was His servant? (Job 42: 7-8):

7   *And it was so, that after the LORD had spoken these words unto Job, the Temanite, My wrath is kindled against thee, and against thy two friends: for ye have not spoken of me the thing that is right, as my servant Job hath.*

8   *Therefore take unto you now seven bullocks and seven rams, and go to my servant Job, and offer up for yourselves a burnt offering; and my servant Job shall pray for you: for him will I accept: lest I deal with you after your folly, in that ye have not spoking of me the thing which is right, like my servant Job.*

In those two verses God mentioned "my servant Job" four times. Despite the temptation, God still recognized Job as his chosen one, because he feared and honoured God, obeyed His commandment, did His will and lived a life that was pleasing unto Him. Hence, God recommended that he had to intercede on behalf of his friends before their offering could be accepted. Nonetheless, all that Job lost was twice restored.

He was a man of authority, wealthy, but Satan in his craftiness went ahead to test his faith in God to see if he would deny God, or would hold to what he believed. He passed the test and was approved by God. He did not seek revenge against his friends because of their bad characters while he was undergoing trials. Saints of God, let's live according to the perfect will of God for Him to be delighted in us.

In some instances when people are hurt, their response is that they will not forgive until they get to heaven before the issues would be resolved. Do you know that no sinner will inherit the Kingdom of Heaven? My life was transformed both personal and ministerial experiences changed my perception towards some human nature, the way they behaved. It was then I realized that unforgiveness is poisonous. I beseech you beloved of God, try as much as possible not to entangle your heart with malice, grudges, nor acting wickedly etc. As you hold someone, so another person will hold you in his/her mind too. Please try to do away with unrighteousness, insincerity, lies, backbiting, gossip etc. May we use our mouths to depopulate the kingdom of darkness, and to propagate the Kingdom of Heaven. You are the epistle people are reading and emulating. Most people don't carry the Bible around, everything is on technology (iPads).

Hence, Job's friend now realized that despite all the trials that Job went through God never forgotten him; their intention must have been, Job was paying for his sins, but God proved to the devil that He is Sovereign when you pass through any challenges of life; He never leaves nor forsakes you. Therefore, God repeatedly declared that "Job was His servant" of the Living God; he was tested and obtained approval. May we attain endorsement from God and whatever challenges you might be going through; God will show Himself and the perfect will of God will manifest in your life.

Another event in regard to the account of

Joseph that led him into captivity by his brethren, what they meant for evil the Lord turned it to good (Genesis 42-46). He was imprisoned due to his master's wife (Potiphar). Nonetheless he never compromised. His gift made room for him, he interpreted the dream for the troubled king, and became the prime minister of Egypt at that time. At long last, the delayed prophecy came to pass, and there was a famine in the land that made the brothers start hunting for food. They finally bowed down for Joseph. He forgave them and cared for them because the Lord defended and fought for him. With all the trials, temptations and challenges, Joseph feared God and showed kindness to his people that sold him into captivity. Joseph did not compromise and was able to love his brothers, he forgave and cared for them. He emulated Christ in doing well, and we ought to do likewise for acceptance.

No wonder King David was declared a man after God's heart. The key word is "Heart of forgiveness". David acknowledged his sin, was able to appease God and never committed the same atrocities or mistakes again. It was then he asked God to cleanse him of all unrighteousness (Psalms 51). We pray that if in any capacity we might have sinned against God, we seek for His mercy and to forgive all our iniquities as we confess from our inner mind in Jesus' mighty name, Amen.

Disobedience

Deliberate the incident of the disobedient prophet (1st Kings 13: 11-32). Leaders should be careful not to lead their members astray or outrank them, while everyone should be conscious of doing as God has commanded and live a pleasing lifestyle. The young prophet was misled, as he was deceived by the older prophet while he dishonoured God. He perceived wrongly, with the notion that the old man had been in the Ministry before him, so he had much experience in the affairs of God. A ministerial calling or God's calling is entirely different; what you heard is different from what someone is advising you to act on. The Lord sent the young prophet on an assignment and gave him instruction not to eat nor drink. It was just for him to obey God's commandment. The young man forgot that the Christian race is a personal race. Through honouring a man of God, the young prophet was deceived by a senior man of God (a prophet) who destroyed his destiny.

Many young lives have been truncated by people who are supposed to be role models or mentors to people seeking achievement in career or ministerial prospects. I pray that we shall not destroy destinies and no one shall destroy ours in Jesus' name. Remember and be assured that you shall give account, be it good or bad, towards people under your authority or whatever vision you have embarked upon. I will recommend you do not compromise; there are many violence within this generation because of position, power, money etc. The Lord is telling us to be kind to one another, and try not to maltreat, mislead or be cruel towards people around you, neither colleagues, nor subordinates nor people under your power. Therefore, I advised that it is time for us to change from ill acts into a new pathway before it is too late, if your works are not in line with the principles of God. Revelation 2:7:

He that hath an ear, let him hear what the Spirit saith unto the churches: To him that overcometh will I give to eat of the tree of life which is in the midst of the paradise of God.

Let's have an insight into the account of Jonah. He was a man of God but a disobedient servant who was displeased because God repented over Nineveh (Jonah 4). Do you notice that in most cases when people are going through challenges, some friends and relatives are happy, and when there is a way of escape they will react negatively? God changed His mind and delivered Nineveh, as they repented from their sins. May the Lord deliver our nation as we stand in the gap interceding, and our lifestyles shall draw men to the Kingdom of Heaven.

Thank God for Naaman, the captain who was cured of leprosy (2nd King 5: 1-14). He initially refused to adhere to the advice given by his servant, but later yielded. He would have missed the opportunity of healing from his infirmity, but in obedience and humility he adhered to the advice, and was cleansed, healed and made whole. The Lord is warning us to be humble, and not to despise people around us. No matter what the level of anybody within your reach, do not despise them. They could be the solution to your problems or the answer to your questions. If you are humble enough, you can learn from anybody.

Jesus entered into the perfect will of God, if not because of His meekness, counting Himself as nothing except a servant to suffer for the perfect will of His Father. Hence, it is essential for us to subdued flesh in order to be a genuine Christian who can obey and do the perfect will of God. However, it takes humility and courage to submit to a servant as captain Naaman did. So also, a genuine pastor/ leader who shepherds churches with passionate members, who believed what they preach, they acted as role models to their disciples as ambassadors of Christ.

"For ye have need of patience, that, after ye have done the will of God, ye might receive the promise" (Hebrews 10:36).

If we truly desire to follow Christ, it is suggested we should abide in Him and endeavour to have an individual bond with Him as He has with His Father. The key role is to have a personal relationship with God only, and that was the epistle written to obtaining the promise of God for acceptance towards His approval. Notwithstanding what the world around us is doing, just because the standards of the world have fallen it does not mean the values of the Church should diminish. Christians are to be the light of the world. We must fight against compromise, aiming to suffer the flesh, and abide to His commandment as a laid-down principle rather than failing to please God.

Chapter Eight

ACCEPTANCE CRITERIA

———◇———

According to the scripture (Mathew 25: 31-46):

31 **When the Son of man shall come in his glory, and all the holy angels with him, then shall he sit upon the throne of his glory.**

32 **And before him shall be gathered all nations: and he shall separate them one from another, as a shepherd divideth his sheep from the goats:**

33 And he shall set the sheep on his right hand, but the goats on the left.

34 Then shall the King say unto them on his right hand, Come, ye blessed of my Father, inherit the Kingdom prepared for you from the foundation of the world.

35 For I was an hungered; and ye gave me meat: I was thirsty, and ye gave me drink; I was a stranger, and ye took me in:

36 Naked, and ye clothed me: I was sick, and ye visited me: I was in prison, and ye came unto me.

37 Then shall the righteous answer him, saying, Lord, when saw we thee an hungered and fed thee? or thirsty, and gave thee drink?

38 When saw we thee a stranger, and took thee in? or naked, and clothed thee?

39 Or when saw we thee sick, or in prison, and came unto thee?

40 And the King shall answer and say unto

them, Verily I say unto you, Inasmuch as ye have done it unto one of the least of these my brethren, ye have done it unto me.

41 Then shall he say also unto them on the left hand, Depart from me, ye cursed, into everlasting fire, prepared for the devil and his angels:

42 For I was an hungered, and ye gave me no meat: I was thirsty, ye gave me no drink:

43 I was a stranger, and ye took me not in: naked, and ye clothed me not: sick, and in prison, and ye visited me not.

44 Then shall they also answer him, saying, Lord, when saw we thee an hungered, or athirst, or a stranger, or naked, or sick, or in prison, and did not minister unto thee?

45 Then shall he answer them, saying, Verily I say unto you inasmuch as ye did it not to one of the least of these, ye did it not to me.

46 And these shall go away into everlasting

punishment: but the righteous into life eternal.

From the above verses are the demonstrations of the judgment towards the nations thus: to God's people who will at the end be standing before Christ He will be the Judge and then, to separate saved believers from the goats representing the lost. The saved are invited to come into the Kingdom to share the blessings of His Kingdom, thus the essence of their acceptance. Therefore, we need to consider if our ways of living are appropriate to the will of God before it is too late. It is for us to make every effort and work toward the ultimate goal of good report as stated below in (verses 23) *His lord said unto him, Well done, good and faithful servant; thou has been faithful over a few things, I will make thee ruler over many things: enter thou into the joy of thy lord.*

This voice of 'well done' shall be the commendation of approval from the Lord as a result of living a life that pleases Him and doing His will. Thereafter declared repeatedly (Revelation 2:29): *He that hath an ear, let him hear what the Spirit saith unto the churches.*

God remained the same and changed not. May God give you the strength and the grace to do as commanded for acceptance in Jesus Mighty Name Amen.

Chapter Nine

WAKE-UP CALL FOR THE CHOSEN/ELECTED SAINTS

———⫸✦⫷———

Christ will not blot the names of his chosen and faithful ones out of the book of life, although men may be attending various denominational churches, baptized in the Holy Ghost, and engage in professions as a means of living. In other words, without a spiritual life, such people often lose their designations before passing away, as they add no value and make no impact to humanity and the Kingdom of Heaven for internal life.

Nevertheless, the names of the overcomers shall never be blotted out. Jesus Christ will present the names of the faithful saints, the chosen ones, where they were inscribed before His Father (John 15:16):

Ye have not chosen me, but I have chosen you, and ordained you, that ye should go and bring forth, fruit, and that your fruit should remain: that whatsoever ye shall ask of the Father in my name, he may give it you.

Having been chosen, how close are you to Him? Heaven defends the chosen believers to a certain extent, but you cannot afford to live like an average Christian. You ask for the grace to live by the rules that govern the elect because you are unique, and have to abide by Heaven's living standards. Evidently the wisest people on earth are those who obeyed His commandment and sought Him with all their heart. In most instances, God tested his people with money and worldly affairs, to see whether we qualified for His creditability.

Revelation 19:7: *Let us be glad and rejoice, and give honour to him: for the marriage of the Lamb is come, and his wife hath made herself ready.*

There are lots of evil practices out there, and while the kingdom of darkness is depopulated, angels in heaven will be celebrating and because of your good deeds hence, Heaven shall rejoice. Thus you are empowered to impact your world, teaching the undiluted doctrine and guiding people, especially our youth, to the right path, because they are the future of the nations. When we try to support the kingdom, thereby having intimacy with God, this makes Him happy.

Isaiah: 41:8: *But thou, Israel, art my servant, Jacob whom I have chosen, the seed of Abraham my friend*.

This was referring to the Servant of God, the chosen one who has intimacy with Him, and the same applies between master and servant. It is an essential requirement to make Heaven, because you were not only called but chosen (Matt. 20:16): *So the last shall be first; and the first last: for many be called, but few chosen.*

From what is happening at this modern age, there are significant signals that are so disheartening, saints need to make every effort to strive and make it to heaven. Therefore, I suggest that we consider and make amendment of any negative characteristics that do not portray the

Kingdom's philosophies. That is why we must not disappoint God over the assignment given to each one of the elects as you were an exceptional creature to Him. Heaven is as real as hell, so it is better to make the rightful choice for internal life.

Mark 13:20: ***And except that the LORD had shortened those days, no flesh should be saved: but for the elect's sake, whom he hath chosen, he hath shortened the days.***

However, according to 1st Peter, 1:10-11

10 *Of which salvation the prophets have inquired and searched diligently, who prophesied of the grace that should come unto you:*

11 *Searching what, or what manner of time the Spirit of Christ which was in them did signify, when it testified beforehand the sufferings of Christ, and the glory that should follow.*

The above verses were highlighting the prophecy of salvation as prophesied in the Old Testament. They desired to know when the Messiah's coming would be and what would be the state of affairs of the second coming of Christ. There is no doubt about the signs which are so glaring (Luke 21:5-

28); they are signs of the end time. The question is: how are you justifying Heaven's certainty? Because any time you deviate from His purpose, it is an indication that you have disappointed Him. I will suggest that believers routinely do self-evaluation considering your lifestyles, thereby being able to bear fruit towards His kingdom.

We shall not be caught unawares like the foolish virgins who were careless and not watchful (Matthew 25:13): *Watch therefore, for ye know neither the day nor the hour wherein the Son of man cometh.*

From the picture of the thief that never gave any notice (1st Thessalonians 5:2): *For yourselves know perfectly that the day of the Lord so cometh as a thief in the night*

That is how the coming of Christ will be. Hence, beloved of God, I will suggest we diligently obey His commandments for the great honour awaiting saints on that glorious day: in doing His will, live a life that pleases Him to obtain His approval.

As repeatedly declared in the book of Revelation (3:22): *He that hath an ear, let him hear what the Spirit saith unto the churches (saints)*

Remember as it was during the time of Noah (Hebrew 11:7), He is still the same:

By faith Noah, being warned of God of things not seen as yet, moved with fear, prepared an ark to the saving of his house; by which he condemned the world, and became heir of the righteousness which is by faith.

My prayer is we shall not be condemned in Jesus' name. As mentioned above, endeavor to live a holy lifestyle that pleases God for an authentic certificate of approval.

Hebrew 13:8: *Jesus Christ the same yesterday, and today, and forever.*

He changes not, for He is a sovereign God.

CONCLUSION

This book is to raise awareness of a wake-up message addressing people of God universally, as He instructed John in his epistles to address designated churches through the angels of the church. God is sovereign. In His kindness He has been sending many men and women of God to let saints consider their ways by living a pleasing lifestyles that will grant believers certificates of approval. Hence, it is applicable to churches of today until the coming of the Lord. As it was during the era of Noah, He is sending messages through His servant, so that none shall be cut without preparation. The repeated phrase is that nobody has any excuse for not making it. I pray that we shall make it to Heaven.

Revelation 3:13: *He that hath an ear, let him hear what the Spirit saith unto the churches*.

This is an alertness for the returning of Christ for His church to be ready.

As you read this book, may you be inspired and transformed in Jesus' Mighty Name Amen. Shalom!

www.ingramcontent.com/pod-product-compliance
Lightning Source LLC
Chambersburg PA
CBHW061431040426
42450CB00007B/997